# Her Story

Nikita Thakur

Invincible Publication Pvt. Ltd.

For permissions, contact:
Invincible Publication Pvt. Ltd.
201A, SAS Tower, Sector 38, Gurugram - 122003
Phone: +91-124-4034247
www.invinciblepublishers.com

Sales Office: -4760-61/23, Basement, Pratap Street,
Ansari Road, Daryaganj, New Delhi - 110002
Email: invinciblepublishers@gmail.com

**Title: HerStory**
**Author: Nikita Thakur**
**Developmental Editor: Raveena Paul**
**ISBN: 978-93-5886-850-0**

This is a work of nonfiction. Every effort has been made to accurately represent the events and individuals featured. In cases where names or identifying details have been changed, it has been done to protect the privacy of individuals.

Printed in India
First Edition: November, 2024

# Contents

# About The Book

In historical records, little was written about women. Most researchers back then were Western men, projecting a white male perspective on the past as well. One of the greatest blunders that these accounts made was with the Indian woman—she was thrown out of context, misunderstood, and misrepresented, leading women's history to be full of myths, half-cooked, and one sided. However, with new evidence and studies coming in, things are starting to change and Her story is beginning to emerge. This book is a recollection of these accounts that shed a new light on women and especially Indian women. Every Indian knows about sati, dowry, jauhar, and the darker side of our past but hardly anyone knows about the side which was not washed away, a side that has stories of Indian culture and people that established groundbreaking standards on women empowerment and gender equality. This book is made from a standpoint acknowledging that everything was not gold in the past, there were problems but not everything was bad too. We have made a sincere attempt to bring the real stories of the women's contribution into shaping India. Hopefully with this book, the readers will get to explore a different perspective from what has been taught to us as "History" of Indian women since time immemorial.

# About The Author

Since 2020, Nikita has built a respected presence on YouTube, producing over 185 videos on topics that touch upon India's social, political, and cultural landscape. Many of her videos focusing on women's issues have resonated deeply with audiences, earning over 3 million views collectively, and gaining appreciation for their depth and a fresh insight. In addition to her work as a content creator, she is the COO of GetsetflyMedia, a talent management firm representing five premium YouTube channels spanning genres from science and geopolitics to sociology.

Recognized among Inc91's "15 Inspiring Women to Look Out For in 2023," she brings a unique perspective shaped by her background in science, which drives her to question biases and dig deeper into overlooked narratives. Thakur's vision is to expand her scope of work, using media as a powerful tool to reach people and drive informed conversations, advocate for equality, and inspire a more thoughtful, inclusive society for future generations.

# CHAPTER 1

## The Forgotten Sapien

## How Narratives Can Change Histories And Half Knowledge Can Destroy Generations?

History is often regarded as a subject that has only to do with cramming dates and events that are of no importance today. However, if you look at the world's most pressing issues their roots can be found in the misinterpretation of history and the hiding of facts that changed the narratives for people.

Take for example the story of the cavemen and cavewomen. The 1800s was a period where a lot of research was done on the prehistoric period. Lots of findings were placed regarding how they lived, hunted, or culturized. But a very important section of society was either forgotten or reduced to the negligible value of just being the seductress, a child bearer of society.

I call her, "the forgotten sapien."

Throughout historical records, there was very little written about what women did. Moreover, the notions that were present in societies during that time were projected onto the past. Most of these researchers were men and were westerners. They completely ignored the cultural contexts of places and communities about which they were writing. They looked at everything from the "western and male bias" and gave us the resulting history which was male oriented and had forgotten all about the women from the past.

It was only after the 1970s when more women started joining the ranks of prehistorians, historians, archaeologists and technicians, that the world of women's history opened itself up.

The revelations it brought, have the power to change what we think of women today. The notions that have made their place in our heads, as to "women are physically weak, they have not played a major role in society", "men and women were always unequal" will all loosen its grip on the society.

One of the greatest blunders that these historical accounts have made is with the **Indian woman.** She has been thrown out of context, out of the pages and is widely misunderstood.

The reinterpretation of these texts have opened doors to a new world, a world where Indian culture had a different take on its women. You might have heard of the "pativrata dharam" but due to these historical gaps, word never came out for the "eka-patnivrata dharam" that our texts, like Srimad-Bhagavatam in verse 9.10.54, so describe. We never heard that before Britishers, "tawaiffs" were well regarded in society, their kothas were considered the centers of learning. Amaresh Misra, while speaking of twaiffs from Lucknow, says that they used to educate children of well born families in the etiquette of zabaan, behavior and the correct attitude. We had barely heard the story of Ramayan from Maa Sita's perspective and we of course never heard of Goddess Aditi who was known to be a fierce and independent force of femininity. The story of Draupadi was turned to be a damsel in distress, however if we look deeper she had the most significant role to play in the legend of Mahabharata. The tale of Indian men, who once worshiped the mother goddesses and regarded females in the same regard.

These stories have been hidden from us. The historians of those times, especially the 1800s, projected their western ideologies and erased one of the important things in writing history, 'the context'. Indian culture was in stark difference to the world and its British writers never understood it. We were shown the worst sides of our culture but never the sides that were good. The truth or atleast a side of it would have almost destroyed the basis of British rule in India, "the white man's burden". This book is not at all meant to erase the oppression women have gone through being subjected to the rules of culture and traditions. However this is a sincere attempt to bring the other side of our history as well, a side that has been completely erased, forgotten and subjected to the darkest shadows of the negative. For life and wisdom do not reside in seeing just one side of the story, they reside in finding the balance between both, finding what to take and what to drop.

There was a time in history that tables took a turn and women became the "forgotten sapien". She was given the mantra of subjugation and the fear that the man was her enemy. But it was not like this since the beginning, societies were born relatively egalitarian, men and women once lived an equal lives. Something changed in the course of history.

And the way it has been told has had a big impact on how women have seen themselves and perceived their roles in society. For a long time, women were made to believe they didn't have a significant history. This made them think they had no choice but to accept the limited roles given to them by society. Without these stories of women's achievements in the past, generations after generations felt the need to constantly prove their worth, to fight to be even considered at the same level to the "first gender". When a group's history is hidden or misrepresented, its members often struggle to see their own potential and capabilities. This issue can be understood by looking at how our collective memory and identities were formed.

The work of modern historians, writers, creators and archaeologists is crucial in correcting these historical misrepresentations. By uncovering and highlighting the roles women played in prehistory, they not only provide a more accurate account of the past but also empower future generations.

We have been seeing ourselves, our lives through the eyes of a male. Probably now it's time to see this world through our own eyes, through the eyes of a Female.

# CHAPTER 2

## "World Moved On And Women Just Watched?"

## Common Notions vs. New Evidence

"Women and men were born unequal." "Since the beginning of human civilization it has been like that. Women reared children, gathered food and men did all the work", this has been the story. "Men ruled the society and women just watched." "Men worked outside and women took care of children and household" but what if I tell you the truth you thought was set in stone since the beginning of human civilization, was maybe the biggest lie told to us by the people who wrote our history?

This notion has now come under a spotlight with new evidence streaming in. Science is slowly unveiling the truth, saying that women were always capable and were never physically inferior to men. Women hunted, just like the men. Some papers have even stated that in fact evolution granted females with much more advantages when it came to works that required stamina and endurance like hunting. They were artists, clan leaders, healers, and huntresses. Even more so, women were highly regarded in their societies, there was not much gender segregation and men and women lived a fairly egalitarian life, respecting each other with a touch of tenderness mutual to both sexes. There was no rivalry among the sexes to overpower each other, they divided their chores equally, performed tasks equally and were regarded in their groups equally.

If I ask your thoughts on the roles of male and female in ancient society, high chances are you would tell the story that history has narrated to you: Men were superior to women. This has been the normal take of almost everyone in society. We have been fed the information that men and women were born unequal and that men were associated with hunting while women used to rear the children and take care of the household because they were weak and couldn't do the 'masculine' chores. This continuous influx of historic perspective has created an impression on the contemporary generation, and the older ones too, and has made them keep women at a lower position of hierarchy beginning right from the pastoral times. But did any of us question this narrative ever, 'Was it really like that? Did the world really move on and women kept watching?'. Were women really inferior to men and therefore held a lower position in the strata? Ever questioned the historical perspective that describes women as shadows of men?

What if I tell you that historians hid an important facet of the pastoral times from all of us? That they didn't put much light on the early women along with their roles and the "inferior women" tag is one big lie that we have been told. What if I tell you that history differed significantly from what we have been taught? What if I tell you that women were never inferior? Yes, you read it right. Studies from different parts of the world have gripped this notion within the ropes of new findings and scientific studies. Modern-day scientific explorations have unveiled the truth, and let me tell you, it is far away from the common notion and questions the very basis of the historical findings.

Contemporary studies have revealed that sexual inequality is actually a modern invention. According to them, it has not been the norm of prehistoric society. In the early historic period, both men and women used to work and shared equal status, and there was no discrimination on the basis of gender.

## Stone Age

Be it a cartoon, a book, or a show, if it is about prehistoric culture, women are given the roles of gatherers and never of hunters. They are portrayed carrying a baby in one arm and food in another. They are shown cooking meals for the families and doing the household chores. You won't find them holding a tool in one hand, running behind an animal that might be equal to or bigger than their size. These descriptions that we see in the form of any video or text have nudged our thoughts in the direction where the destination is a 'weak woman'.

But this is far away from the truth. This is actually the opposite of what was the reality at that time, when women were the 'better half' of men in every sense. This is about the time when the human race had not sown the seeds for crops—the time when survival was an absolute necessity and both sexes knew no discrimination.

During the Palaeolithic era, sapiens were involved in the art of hunting animals and gathering food. This was the time when agriculture was not known to them, and they had to rely on daily hunting to feed themselves. The resources that the population relied upon were very limited, and this scarcity necessitated the involvement of both sexes-male and female-for a cooperative approach mandating them to hunt irrespective of the gender

Anthropologists for a long time have supported the idea of men alone being involved in hunting, giving the pretext of them being naturally more aggressive and their build being stronger than women. They have been of the idea that women, because of their slow pace, were better suited for the gathering functions. This notion was questioned during the excavations that were carried out in Peru in 2018. A team of archaeologists in Peru, while examining a burial, found something that came as a big question mark on the century-long belief. They found fragments of cranium teeth and leg bones of a woman, and alongside they also found a

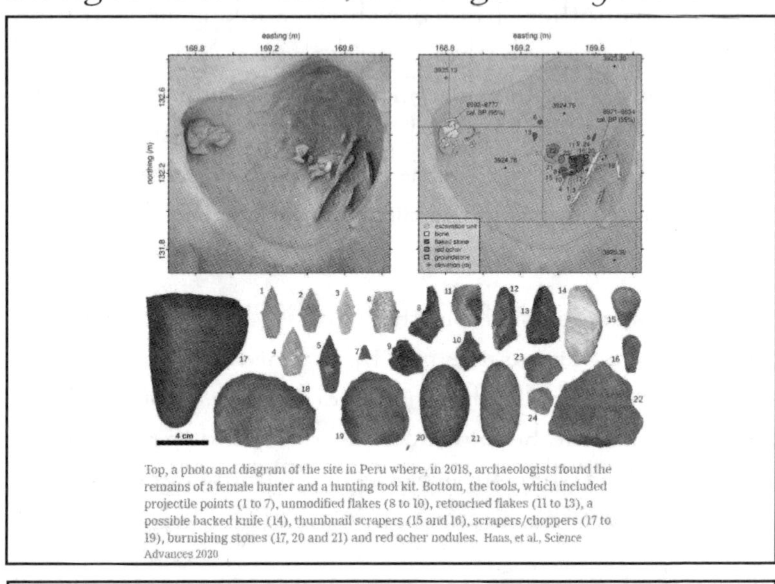


Top, a photo and diagram of the site in Peru where, in 2018, archaeologists found the remains of a female hunter and a hunting tool kit. Bottom, the tools, which included projectile points (1 to 7), unmodified flakes (8 to 10), retouched flakes (11 to 13), a possible backed knife (14), thumbnail scrapers (15 and 16), scrapers/choppers (17 to 19), burnishing stones (17, 20 and 21) and red ocher nodules. Haas, et al., Science Advances 2020

Excavations at the Wilamaya Patjxa archaeological site in Peru, where the nearly 10,000-year-old remains of a female hunter was found in 2018. Randall Haas

Image Source- The New York Times

hunting kit with more tools like scrapers, projectile points, flakes, and burnishing stones.

With this excavation, all the previous tools, which were discovered by archaeologists at different sites, made sense. A 1963 excavation in Colorado, where remains of a woman were found alongside a projectile pointer buried with her. The male centric ideology concluded that that tool was merely used as a scraping knife and had no connection with hunting.

These buried tools are of great significance, and they speak a lot about the ancient times. During the stone age, when people died, they were buried with all their belongings. These excavations thereby uncovered the truth, which was veiled by biased historians who projected the present onto the past as well.

There was another study that combed through the Database of Places, Languages, Culture, and Environment, which is a catalog of ethnographies about human societies in the 19th and 20th centuries.

Dr. Wall-Scheffler and her students conducted a thorough examination of 63 societies that thrived during the 19th and 20th centuries, including the Bakola of Southern Cameroon and the Hadza of Tanzania, among others. Their research revealed compelling evidence of women's participation in hunting across 50 of these societies. Lardil, Cree, Inuit, Maidu, and Central Eskimo.

This study even unveiled that women had a flexible approach to hunting that kept changing as they aged.

Apart from the archaeological evidence that we discussed, we also have physiological evidence that supports women's role as hunters in the prehistoric times.

The study conducted by researchers from various U.S. universities, as detailed in the journal **American Anthropologist**, presents physiological evidence underscoring that hunting was a collective endeavor. Their examination of injuries found on both male and female bodies revealed striking similarities, emphasizing a crucial point: both genders were engaged in comparable types of labor.

support this claim further, we have another research paper published by Cara Ocobock. In this paper, Cara has highlighted the studies of early human fossils that revealed a number of traumatic injuries. The injuries observed in prehistoric women, such as head and chest injuries or fractures, are similar to those experienced by modern rodeo clowns, who often suffer from being kicked by animals or attacked. These types of injuries suggest that women, like men, engaged in dangerous, close-contact hunting practices, which involved ambushing large game animals.

Researchers also found that both men and women displayed similar rates of wear and tear on their bodies, indicating that hunting was not a gendered activity in these prehistoric societies. Therefore, we can say that Sexual division of labor was nearly absent, and females were equally participative in every aspect.

With all the above evidence, one must think, 'What made the women in the ancient past undertake physically straining and hectic tasks such as hunting?' Well, it was because of the hormones. Yes, you read it right, hormones! Now you might think that how were hormones supporting females as hunters?

Let's understand this. Till date, various studies have been carried out that deal with the roles of hormones in prehistoric women and these studies pretty much question the male centric view.

As per a study conducted by Cara Ocobock and Sarah Lacy , estrogen, a hormone predominantly found in female bodies, binds to estrogen receptors—structures that are historically more ancient than testosterone receptors, which facilitate the binding of testosterone in males. Research by Joseph Thornton and his colleagues at the University of Chicago suggests that estrogen receptors date back approximately 1.2 billion to 600 million years, making them roughly twice as old as their testosterone counterparts.

Beyond its role in regulating the reproductive system, estrogen influences fine motor control and memory, promotes neuronal growth and development, and helps prevent arterial hardening. It also plays a vital role in enhancing fatty acid oxidation while reducing glycogen utilization and increasing insulin sensitivity.

The elevation of fatty acid oxidation provides an alternative energy source to glycogen, thereby supporting sustained physical activity during endurance exercises. Increased insulin sensitivity, in turn, facilitates greater glucose uptake by muscles, further bolstering endurance performance.

When on a hunt, women had to run for hours, and here estrogen used to play its role.

Additionally, adiponectin is another critical hormone found in higher concentrations in females than in males. This hormone enhances fat metabolism while conserving carbohydrates for future use and protecting muscle tissue from breakdown. According to a study by Anne

Friedlander of Stanford University and her colleagues, females utilize as much as 70 percent more fat for energy during exercise compared to their male counterparts.

Therefore, these hormones allowed women to undertake long and physically straining tasks like hunting in the prehistoric times.

Another factor that allowed women to hunt was their typically wide hip structure which allowed women to rotate their hips properly. This hip-to-hip movement supported them to take longer steps, preventing their energy and making the activity metabolically cheaper for them.

All these studies therefore point towards one thing—women were hunters too! They support the idea that women were equally involved in the task of hunting and were not limited to gathering only.

## Parenting: A Non-Biased And Communal Role

The parenting style of prehistoric tribes was very different from what it looks like in the modern world. Studies have even shown that children in ancient times were more emotionally and physically connected to their tribes.

The stone age stood true to the popular saying 'it takes a village to raise a child'. When a child was born, the whole village joined in to parent her/him. A recent study titled 'Sensitive Responsiveness and Multiple Caregiving Networks Among Mbendjele BaYaka Hunter-Gatherers: Potential Implications for Psychological Development and Well-Being' has thrown light on the same. BaYaka is a semi-nomadic tribe in the Democratic Republic of the Congo, and the study was carried out by anthropologists from Cambridge University.

The study revealed that the style of parenting and caregiving found in the hunter-gathering tribes is more likely to result in healthy psychological development. This is because in these tribes the concept of community parenting is prevalent. Apart from the biological parents, all the members of the community are active players in the rearing and caring of the child. This makes the infant feel continuous human touch, a major lacking in modern parenting styles.

The physical contact and caregiving available to the child throughout the day ensured that the child got approximately nine hours of close contact from every member of the tribe. It was because the children were carried by the carer either on their back using a sling or were held in the carer's front. Given the clothing style or attire carried out by the tribes, the majority of this contact was a skin to skin type of contact which is acknowledged by medical professionals for a range of physical and emotional advantages. These include the regulation of the baby's heart rate, breathing, and enhanced brain development.

Apart from the positive impact on the child, mothers were highly benefited with such a practice. The involvement of the community provided the mother enough time to take rest, which is indeed important for a new mother. They used to get enough sleep and thereby energy to complete their chores.

Today, we sapiens have "evolved," but during this course we have seen some golden practices fading away. Thanks to the studies that are being carried out with scientific backing, we are able to trace the lost historical gems—that we got to know the concept of community parenting and how it favored female wellbeing and children's development both.

## Were The First Artists Women?

Historians for a long time have been relying on the remains from history to uncover different aspects of that time. They have been involved in excavation activities, carbon dating, examining the artifacts, and more. Cave paintings have been a reliable source for exploring the ancient truths, as these are the only records that are distantly close to writing of any kind for this period. The understanding of the images that were painted on the walls by the people who prevailed on this planet centuries ago gives us a holistic view of that time. The presence of animal figures in the caves and certain human figures speaks about the nature of that era.

Photo - Handprints in ancient cave art
Source- National Geographic

But the question was, who made these paintings?

The male-centric approach has been crowning the men of that time for these historic heritages. For example, R. Dale Guthrie, one of the scholars in this field had previously suggested that most of these handprints were made by adolescent boys, who explored caves out of curiosity and drew images reflecting their interests, such as naked women and dangerous animals.

Since the beginning, when the examination of these stencils began, a male-dominated narrative has emerged, portraying these paintings as artifacts exclusively crafted by men. These hand stencils featured depictions of animals such as bison, reindeer, and horses which are traditionally attributed to "male hunters". These images were thought to serve as records of their kills or as part of some "hunting magic" aimed at enhancing future success. This prevailing view, lived on for too long, perpetuated by biased archaeologists, stating that men were the first artists.

However, this can be far from the truth.

It all started with John Manning, a British biologist. Manning studied these paintings and explained that these first artists might actually have been women because of the size of the fingers in the handprints. He argued that the women's ring and index finger are of almost the same length, but it differs in the case of men. For males, the ring finger is longer than the index finger. And in this case these handprints appeared to resemble a female hand.

Then came archaeologist Dean Snow of Pennsylvania State University and he, taking after John Manning, analyzed hand stencils found in caves. Stencils and prints have been discovered in caves worldwide, including locations in Argentina, Africa, Borneo, and Australia, but the most well-known examples are from southern France and northern Spain, dating between 12,000 and 40,000 years ago. He shortlisted eight cave sites in France and Spain. While Snow reviewed numerous stencils from these caves, only 32 were clear enough to measure because others were either faded or smudged: 16 from Spain's El Castillo, 6 from France's Gargas, and 5 from Pech Merle.

Following Manning's work, Snow also pulled out a 40-year-old book about cave paintings from his shelf. Upon seeing a colorful hand stencil from the Pech Merle cave in southern France, Snow thought to himself, "Man, if Manning knows what he's talking about, then this is almost certainly a female hand."

After this, Snow developed an algorithm to differentiate male and female handprints, based on measurements of hand proportions from modern people of European descent. These factors included the length of fingers and ratios between the ring, index, and little fingers. Although the algorithm had only about 60% accuracy for contemporary hands—due to similarities between male and female characteristics—Snow discovered that prehistoric hands were far more sexually dimorphic, meaning that they had very distinctive differences which made it easy to differentiate the male and female hand in them. As he put it, "Twenty thousand years ago, men were men and women were women."

Dean Snow and his team found that the majority—around 75% of handprints in prehistoric caves paintings—belonged to women. Signifying that women, in fact, might have been the first artists of our world.

However, this research has opened up more questions which are yet to be answered.

There are some scholars such as archaeologist Dave Whitley, who welcome Snow's findings as a significant contribution. Whitley, unlike Guthrie, believed that the cave art was likely created by shamans who entered altered states of consciousness. In many hunter-gatherer societies, shamans are mostly women or even transgender individuals, reasserting the point made by Snow.

Now some questions remain unanswered, Why were women responsible for the majority of these handprints? Did they create only the hand stencils, or all the artwork? However, this new journey is a long one.

The discovery of predominantly female handprints in these ancient caves challenges previous assumptions about gender roles in early societies, offering fresh perspectives on the cultural and spiritual significance of prehistoric art.

## Coming Up Of The Agriculture

A study led by Mark Dyble reveals that early human societies, particularly those of hunter-gatherers, may have been founded on principles of equality between men and women. Dyble's research suggests that sexual equality wasn't a recent development but instead played a crucial role in shaping human evolution. In contemporary hunter-gatherer tribes, decisions such as where to live and who to live with were often made jointly by men and women, which resulted in communities that were not dominated by any one gender. This social structure is thought to have fostered survival advantages by allowing for broader social networks and greater cooperation between unrelated individuals

But Dyble and his colleagues found that once agriculture emerged, these egalitarian principles began to fade. The hunter-gatherer groups, which often comprised about 20 individuals and allowed for equal influence of both sexes, began to shrink to much smaller groups of about six after the advent of farming. This shift was rooted in the fundamental change in labor dynamics. In the pre-agricultural period, men and women contributed relatively equally to the survival of the group, with both sexes providing essential resources such as hunting animals, gathering fruits, or honey. This balance meant women had a significant voice in decisions, and as a result, larger and more interconnected social networks emerged. These networks allowed early humans to avoid inbreeding and share innovations, which would have been crucial for survival and social cohesion.

However, with the rise of agriculture, societies became more male-dominated. Farming allowed people to accumulate resources, and men, in particular, began to form tight alliances with male kin. This shift resulted in male-dominated social hubs and decreased the influence of women in societal decision-making. The need for survival cooperation with unrelated individuals, which was essential in hunter-gatherer societies, diminished. As men began to accumulate wealth and form alliances to protect their assets, women's roles were reduced, particularly as the physical need for hunting lessened with the increasing reliance on cultivated crops.

This agricultural revolution significantly altered social dynamics, creating a male-centric structure where men could accumulate wealth, take multiple wives, and form stronger familial ties with their male relatives. The role of women in decision-making, once critical for group survival, became more limited as their contributions were no longer perceived as crucial to the same degree. Consequently, women's societal position was downgraded, marking a clear contrast to the earlier egalitarian norms of the hunter-gatherer era.

After the last ice age and the coming up of the Neolithic period, sapiens shifted their mode of survival, and they began domesticating animals and growing crops. This transition is also called the Neolithic Agricultural Revolution.

The shift from hunting to agriculture provided a wider window of resources. Humans now had the leverage to quit hunting, which was a hectic task, and adopt agriculture. Males in society came to the forefront in agriculture. They were involved in almost every aspect of the activities.

The contemporary world is an evolved society. The human race has seen a lot of changes in both the geography of their place and their own physiology as well. With time, we saw the emergence of more settled societies rather than the earlier hunter-gatherers. Then we saw a shift that brought the settlements of civilizations. Slowly and steadily, we as humans moved from one step to another, evolving into a newer version of ourselves. But in between this evolution, we almost forgot the true roots of our existence. The problem emerged when we completely moved on from the established facts that women were actually more than what they have been perceived as. The studies that we discussed are important to unveil the reality that we have missed out on. We are not told that women were the huntersess, that they were probably even the first artists, that men and women shared equal roles and responsibilities and that raising a child was a community affair and that's what the truth is.

These findings add to a growing body of evidence that women in the Stone Age were engaged in a much broader range of activities than traditionally assumed. To conclude, the Stone Age societies remind us of a time when survival took precedence over divisions based on gender roles. Emerging evidence from archaeological finds and physiological research reveals that women, like men, were actively engaged in hunting and contributed equally to their communities in various roles, including caregiving, creating art, and sustaining family life. These findings challenge long standing beliefs and demonstrate that strength, creativity, and resilience have always been shared traits across humanity.

Rather than assigning fixed roles, the Palaeolithic era appears to have valued adaptability, skill, and collaboration, with both women and men playing vital, interchangeable roles in hunting, gathering, nurturing, and creating. Each individual contributed to the collective success, underscoring that survival was a shared journey of resilience, resourcefulness, and ingenuity.

As we reflect on these early societies, let's embrace the idea that strength and creativity are human qualities, not bound to one gender. The Stone Age offers a powerful reminder of a shared history of cooperation, highlighting the benefits of valuing every member of society equally in the face of life's challenges.

# CHAPTER 3

## The First Feminist Culture

Thousands of years ago there was a civilization that exemplified the definition of equality in the world. They presented in example how modern societies could function without gender differences, religion, authority and violence. Equality and especially gender equality was never foreign to India, it originated here. The first urban civilization of what we know today as India, started with the cult of mother goddesses, signifying the place that women held in their society.

Some scholars tell us that Indus valley civilization was not just the first urban civilization of India but it could also be of the world dating back at least three-four thousand years.

This civilization that survived for 5,000 years held its Females high and recognized the third gender. Sex was not a taboo for them. The topic was discussed openly and shown through figurines in the public forum. We are talking here about The Indus Valley Civilization. It was a complex network of at least 1500 towns and cities spread over 680,000 sq. kilometers of land.

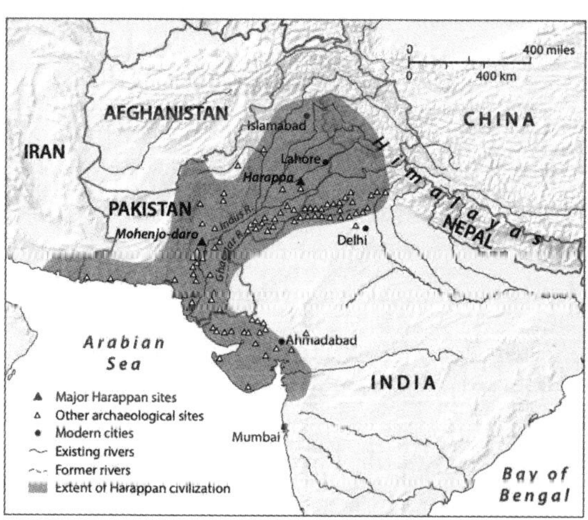


Image- The Indus Valley Civilization

These towns represented each facet of a modern society; city planning, water systems, drainage, settlements everything screamed of modernity but with equality. The artifacts they left behind tell a story of a society unafraid to embrace the essence of humanity, where fertility and love were honored without shame. Figurines depicting male and female sexuality stand testament to a culture that cherished the natural rhythms of life, that saw the act of sex as a miracle, something greater than themselves and may be even sacred. The things that appear to be a utopian world for our modern times, were reality in the times of this civilization. During the colonial period Britishers had often painted the image of Indians as barbaric, uncivilized and through clear manipulation we were made to accept each brunt on our culture, being brainwashed into believing that India never knew how to be modern and egalitarian. They created this narrative that it was them who taught us about equality in terms of civil society and even in terms of gender. But if we look back at our history, since the beginning of our civilizations, our culture was founded upon the liberal themes. For them equality was not an ideal but the reality of society.

100 years have been spent on thoroughly studying the indus valley civilization and till date the discoveries have just pointed towards an egalitarian society that was advanced and far more modern than its contemporaries, the Egyptian and the Mesopotamian civilization.

## Proofs Through Archeological Evidence

In the ancient land of Harappa, a thriving civilization flourished along the banks of the Indus River. Its people built impressive cities, traded with faraway lands, and crafted beautiful art. Among their many achievements, the people of Harappa also left behind terracotta figurines, small sculptures made from clay, which told stories of their beliefs, their way of life, and perhaps even their views on gender and society. Indus valley civilization didn't leave much written records for us. Whatever written we have, belongs to a script which has not been deciphered as of now. So, whatever we know of this civilization is through the archaeological evidence that has been left behind. One of the primary subjects of archaeological evidence is figurines. These figurines offer a fascinating window into how the Harappans may have understood and celebrated the roles of men, women, and those who didn't fit neatly into either category.[1]

## The Power Of Women In Harappa

Figurines of Harappa give us clues about the roles of women in society. While many of the figurines depict women as mothers, with large breasts and wide hips, only a few show them with infants. This suggests that while motherhood was important, it wasn't the only role women played in society. Women in Harappa may have been much more than caretakers—they were also involved in the economic and spiritual life of the community.

1. **Rita P. Wright:** Wright, in her book "The Ancient Indus: Urbanism, Economy, and Society," discusses the evidence of gender equality in the Indus Valley Civilization, including the prominence of female figurines and the absence of clear evidence of gender-based social hierarchy.

Image- Female figurine holding a nursing infant from Harappa
Source- Shindhishaan - voice of the sindh

Image- Figurine from Indus Valley Civilization of a women
Source- Research paper by Jithin R. Veer

Fig. 1.5 **Female figurine from the Indus Valley.** Images such as this terra-cotta statuette from the Indus Valley Civilization were perhaps representations of goddesses who were worshiped for their live-giving powers. (Photo: Bildarchiv Preussischer Kulturbesitz / Art Resource, N.Y.)

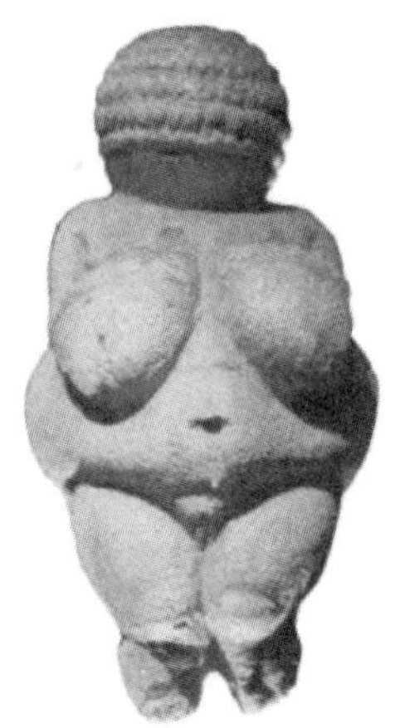

Fig. 1.6 **The Venus of Willendorf.** This figurine from Northern Europe is one example of an ancient goddess who some believe may have been at one time the object of worldwide devotion. (Photo courtesy of Creative Commons, Matthias Kabel.)

One of the most interesting things about Harappan women is their association with fertility and prosperity. In the paper 'A Glimpse at the Human Figurines of the Indus Valley Civilization' by Jithin R. Veer, some figurines show women with exaggerated features, such as large hips and bellies, which may symbolize their role in ensuring the fertility of the land and the abundance of crops as women were seen as creative forces that brought fertility on earth. In this way, the women of Harappa were seen as powerful figures, capable of ensuring the survival and prosperity of their people.

Then the detailed craftsmanship and elaborate ornamentation of the figurines from Harappa and Mohenjo-daro provide fascinating insights into the possible status of women in the Indus Valley Civilization. The fact that these figurines are adorned with layers of necklaces, chokers, and elaborate headdresses indicates that women held an important and possibly revered place in society.

Image-Figurine from Harappar. This figurine can be seen wearing three sets of choker and necklace along with the common fan shaped headdress with cups on either side of the head.

Source- Research paper by Jithin R. Veer

Image- Female figurine with painted ornaments from Harappa

Source- Research paper by Jithin R. Veer

The attention to their attire and accessories suggests that women, or at least the ones these figurines represent, may have enjoyed a high social status or been symbols of wealth, fertility, or divinity. There is even evidence to suggest that women were involved in the production of goods like pottery and faience, a type of glazed ceramic that was highly prized in the ancient world. This means that women likely contributed to the economic engine of Harappan society, not just through domestic tasks but by engaging in larger-scale production and trade.

Some of the figurines, like the one with the fan-shaped headdress that might have served as a sacred lamp, hint at the possibility that women were connected to religious or ritual practices. This suggests that women could have been involved as priestesses or key figures in rituals.

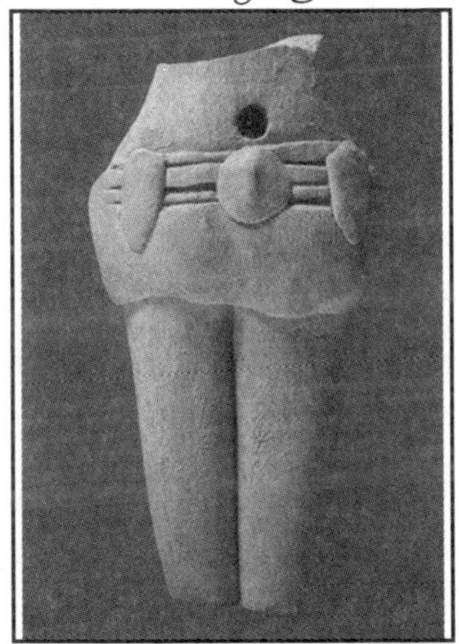

Image- A multi strap belt on some female figurine
Source- Research paper by Jithin R. Veer

These figurines were made in a careful and elaborate way—with ornaments applied separately and the use of both terracotta and bronze—shows that women were depicted with great care and respect. The fact that special techniques like lost-wax casting were used for some of the bronze figures implies that women, or their symbolic representation, were considered worthy of exceptional artistic effort.

The fact that similar jewelry to what is found on the figurines has been uncovered in hoards suggests that women had access to, or were closely associated with, wealth and luxury items. Jewelry has often been a marker of status, and the presence of it on these figurines may indicate that women in certain social classes could afford wealth and prestige. The existence of bronze sculptures, which are distinct from the more common terracotta ones, suggests that women in some communities or groups may had a particular status or role that warranted a different, more durable artistic medium. These figures may have represented women of higher standing or those involved in specific rituals or ceremonies, highlighting the possibility of social or ethnic stratification.

Overall, these figurines point toward a society where women were not only central to domestic life but also likely had a significant social, religious, or even political status, at least in some contexts. The artistry and symbolism suggest that women were respected and perhaps even venerated in certain aspects of Indus Valley life.

Then there are ancient seals from Harappa and Mohenjo-daro that depict such mysterious figures, especially involving tigers and goddesses. One of the most captivating seals, housed at the National Museum in Karachi, shows a human figure with a double bun hairstyle holding onto a tree while gesturing toward a tiger that's looking back at them. It's like there's some unspoken communication or power dynamic between the figure and the tiger, but what it means and the gender of the double bun figure is still up for debate.

And then we have the molded tablet from the Harappa

Image- A female interacting with tigers
Source- Speakingtree.in

Museum, which depicts a fierce female figure battling two tigers while standing on an elephant. Some have interpreted this as Indra riding Airavata, his mythical elephant, or as possibly representing India's first tiger goddess. The figure is part human, part tiger—almost like a sphinx—with her upper half adorned with a headdress and bangles, and her lower half resembling a tiger. This image of a woman fused with a tiger might be the oldest of its kind in the world.

Image- Indus Narrative Tablets
Source- Research paper by Naga Ganesan

**Figure:** molded tablet showing a female deity battling two tigers and standing above an elephant. A single Indus script depicting a spoked wheel is above the head of the deity. Discovered in Harappa, 1997.

There's another seal that shows a woman separating two men who appear to be fighting using trees. The woman, wearing bangles on both arms, stretches them out as she keeps the men apart. This recurring imagery of tigers, women, and battle scenes seems deeply embedded in Harappan lore, though much of the specific meaning has been lost to time.

The depiction of a bird-like goddess holding two tigers apart on yet another seal, and a woman with horns fighting a tiger with horns, all point to some forgotten mythology or ritual involving powerful female figures and tigers. It seems that tigers, especially in the form of these tiger goddesses, played a significant role in Harappan beliefs.

Interestingly, villagers in India today still tell stories of tiger gods and goddesses, which seem to echo these ancient images. People living in forests have developed rich oral traditions involving them, which may be rooted in these ancient depictions.

What's truly puzzling is that these scenes don't have any direct parallels in the mythology we're familiar with today—whether from Aryan or Dravidian traditions. This leaves us wondering: who exactly was this tiger goddess? The seals leave us with clues but no definitive answers. Some suggest the figures represent early goddesses, perhaps even warriors or protectors. However, we still lack a satisfactory explanation that ties all these pieces together.

## Women And Wealth

In Harappa, wealth was not just about money—it was also about fertility, food, and prosperity. Women were often seen as the keepers of this wealth, as their ability to bear children and manage households was directly tied to the survival and success of the community. But beyond this, there is evidence that women may have also managed other forms of wealth, including land and resources.

Some scholars suggest that the richly adorned female figurines of Harappa represent women who played important roles in managing wealth and overseeing economic activities. These women were not just passive recipients of wealth—they were active participants in the economic life of the community. In fact, their status and power may have been tied directly to their ability to control resources and ensure the prosperity of their families.

A research paper by Shary R. Clark suggests one particularly fascinating idea that women in Harappa may have been involved in larger-scale economic production, such as pottery-making and trade. The production of goods like pottery and faience were essential to the economy of Harappa, and it is possible that women played a central role in these industries. If this is true, it would mean that women in Harappa were not confined to domestic tasks but were active contributors to the economy.[2]

## Matrilocality: A Society Where Women Were Central

There is also evidence to suggest that Harappan society may have been matrilocal, meaning that when couples married, the husband would come to live with the wife's family. In such societies, property and inheritance are often passed down through the female line, giving women significant power and authority within the family structure.

This idea stemmed from what scholars are starting to uncover about burial practices at Harappa. So, they've been analyzing genetic traits of the people buried in the same cemetery, and some early results are suggesting that many of the women may have been related to each other, while the men weren't as closely connected. It's like women were being buried near their mothers and grandmothers, but men seemed to be buried with their wife's family rather than their own.[3]

2. **Jonathan Mark Kenoyer:** Kenoyer, a prominent archaeologist specializing in the Indus Valley Civilization, has written extensively about the role of women in ancient Indus society. He suggests that women may have held positions of authority and responsibility, based on archaeological findings of their participation in economic activities and presence in religious iconography.

3. **Gregory L. Possehl:** Possehl, in his work "The Indus Civilization:

If this idea of matrilocal burial—where men join the wife's family—holds up with more research, it could really change the way we understand gender roles in ancient Harappan society. Traditionally, we think of early civilizations as patriarchal, but this would point to a much different dynamic, where women may have had a central role in family and social structures.

If Harappa was indeed a matrilocal society, this would suggest that women held considerable social and economic power. They would have been the heads of their households, with control over property and resources. This kind of social structure is a far cry from the patriarchal societies that dominated much of recorded history, where women had little say in important matters.

In a matrilocal society, women's roles would have extended far beyond the home. They would have been involved in making decisions about land, resources, and the future of their families. This would have given them a level of authority and influence that was unusual for women in many ancient cultures.[4]

This concept of matrilineal society is present in today's India as well. Though not exactly similar to what was there in prehistoric times, women centric societies are present in some parts of India even today. For example, the Khasi tribe of Meghalaya which is also found in Assam,

A Contemporary Perspective," explores various aspects of Indus Valley society, including gender relations. He proposes that the presence of female figurines and the absence of evidence for male dominance in burials indicate a relatively egalitarian society, possibly with elements of matrilineality.

4. **Jane McIntosh:** McIntosh, in her book "The Ancient Indus Valley: New Perspectives," discusses the evidence for gender equality in the Indus Valley Civilization and suggests that women may have played significant roles in both domestic and public spheres.

Tripura and Mizoram in small settlements. In the Khasi community, children inherit the last name of their mother. Their customary laws support the inheritance of property by females only. In this community, daughters are given the liberty, they can choose to live in their ancestral house or move out; but for the youngest daughter, who is called as **ka khadduh** and is also the custodian of the property, she never leaves home. Even after her marriage, she looks after her parents and eventually becomes the head of the household after her mother's death. Similar rules are also found in the Jaintia community, where children inherit the last name of their mother and women are the heirs of the ancestral property. Another example is present in the southernmost island of Lakshadweep which is Minicoy. There are traces of a matrilineal society in small pockets of the island.

Then, in the same line, we also have the presence of Nairs and Mappiles of Kerala. Here, descent is through the lineage of women and succession of property was from mother to daughter.

Strange right? In a society where patriarchy holds strong roots, we still have these handful of examples where the essence of matrilineal society is still present.

## "Embracing Fluidity: Gender And Spirituality In Harappan Society"

The figurines of Harappa, with their curious mixture of male and female features, tell stories of a world where gender was not always viewed in black and white. There are figurines of men wearing skirts and jewelry typically associated with women. Some have no clear male or female characteristics, leaving scholars to wonder about their purpose and meaning. What do these mysterious figures tell us about how the people of Harappa viewed gender, and what can they teach us about women's roles in this ancient civilization?

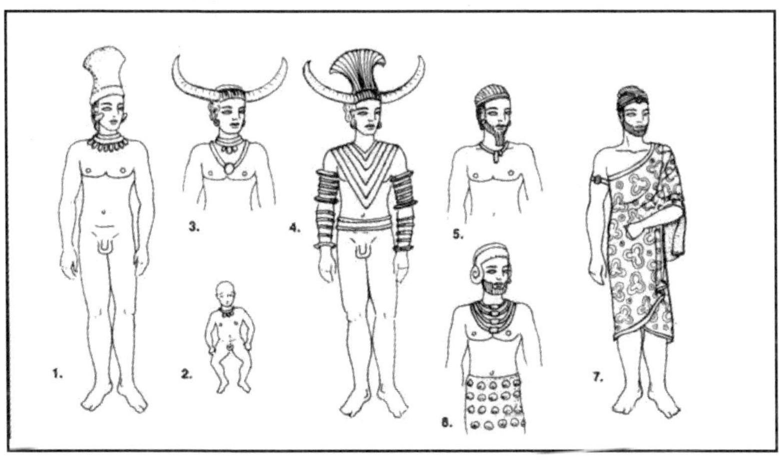

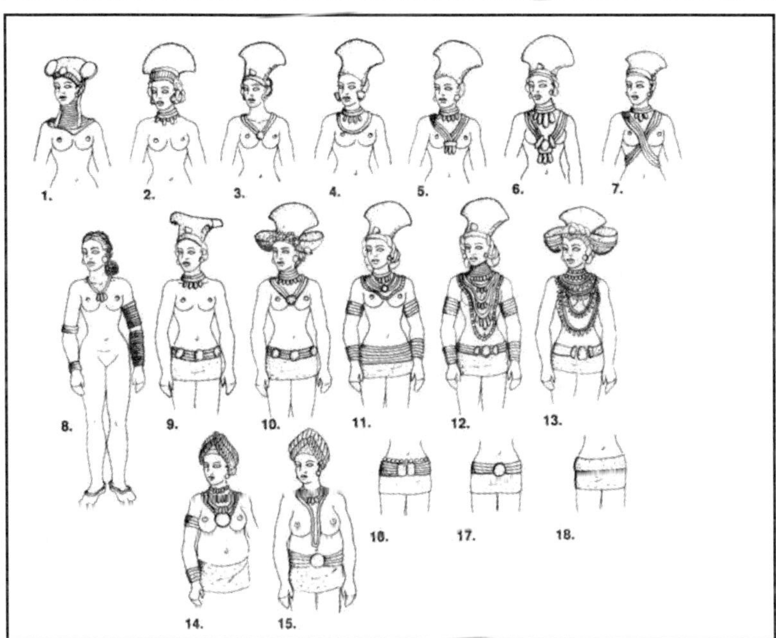

Image Source- Research paper by J.M. Kenoyer

Research by Sharri R. Clark highlights the compelling example of acceptance of gender fluidity in Harappan society, challenging rigid notions of gender. Evidence from terracotta figurines suggests that the people of Harappa did not perceive gender as fixed, but rather as a spectrum where individuals could embody both male and female traits. This perspective reflects an empowering view of gender, highlighting the community's appreciation for diversity and the strength derived from embracing both masculine and feminine qualities.

Integral to this understanding are the androgynous figures, believed to represent shamans or spiritual leaders who transcended traditional gender roles. These individuals, often depicted in clothing that combined male and female elements, were seen as possessing unique spiritual powers. Their ability to navigate the realms of both genders allowed them to communicate with the divine, perform crucial rituals, and foster a connection between the human and the sacred.

Additionally, a subset of figurines with mixed attributes reinforces the idea of a third gender in Harappan culture. These figures, often male or androgynous, donned feminine attire, suggesting a recognition of diverse gender expressions. The design choices, such as obscuring male genitalia or showcasing female characteristics, indicate an inclusive approach to gender roles, accommodating hermaphrodites, androgyny, and cross-dressing.

Moreover, the depiction of women's figurines with short skirts and bare chests, alongside representations of sexual activity and procreation, further illustrates the community's acceptance of varied expressions of gender and sexuality. Such artifacts signify that the people of Harappa embraced a multifaceted understanding of gender, celebrating the fluidity and complexity of human identity.

The Harappan figurines, with their mixture of male and female traits, suggest that ancient cultures like Harappa may have recognized and even celebrated gender diversity. This aligns with contemporary views that gender is not a rigid binary but a spectrum, where individuals can embody various aspects of masculinity, femininity, or neither.

The Harappan acceptance of androgyny and third-gender figures reflects a culture that may have seen gender as fluid, something that could be transcended, particularly in spiritual or ritual contexts. In modern times, many cultures, including Indigenous and non-Western societies, have recognized similar non-binary or third-gender roles (such as hijras in South Asia, two-spirit people in Native American cultures, or kathoey in Thailand). These roles historically gave transgender and gender-nonconforming individuals respected positions within their societies.

The Harappan example shows that gender diversity is not a modern invention but part of human history, one that transcends time and cultural boundaries. It reflects the potential for a broader understanding of gender that honors individual identity and expression, much like the efforts made today to ensure equal recognition and respect for transgender people.

## Indus Valley Vs Other Ancient Civilizations

When we look at the figurines from Harappa, we can see a society that was more complex and diverse than we might have imagined. Gender roles were probably not fixed, and women played important roles in the economic, social, and spiritual life of the community. The presence of androgynous figures, women in positions of power, and a possible matrilocal society suggests that Harappa was a place where women were respected and empowered.

Though much about Harappa remains a mystery, the clues left behind in its figurines tell a story of a society where women held important positions of power and respect. Archaeological findings, such as depictions on seals and figurines, as well as the discovery of tools and artifacts associated with tasks like weaving, pottery-making, and food processing, suggest that women were actively involved in crafts and trade.

Besides gender equality, research has shown that The Indus Valley Civilization stands out for its remarkable social organization, especially when compared to other ancient urban centers like Mesopotamia and Egypt. While these civilizations displayed distinct hierarchies, the Indus Valley was more egalitarian, both in terms of gender and social structures.

1. **Lack of Hierarch:** Unlike Mesopotamia and Egypt, where large palaces and grand structures signified elite status, the Indus valley civilization was comparatively uniform. The absence of palatial residence and equally accessible drainage indicates that society was more equitable in nature. One striking feature of the civilization was the presence of a citadel, an upraised platform generally located on the western side of the region. This citadel was a fortified structure and the one present at Mohenjo-daro marked the presence of the great bath and other structures like granary and even bathrooms. It is believed that the citadel was generally occupied by the people who used to manage the lower town, where people resided, but the

great bath was accessible to all and has been used for ritualistic bathing. This non-discriminatory approach and accessibility of the great bath further strengthen the idea of a more equal society.

Image- The Great Bath of Mohenjo daro
Source- Britannica

Additionally, the absence of structures clearly identified as temples or palaces in the archaeological record have led some scholars, including Jarrige, to propose that the society may have been relatively egalitarian, with power and authority distributed across various individuals rather than concentrated in the hands of a few elites.

2. **Communities made decisions:** The Indus Valley did not exhibit signs of centralized rule, such as palaces or elite tombs. Instead, the lack of aristocratic burials or monumental structures dedicated to rulers points toward a heterarchical system, where power was distributed, and decisions were likely made collectively. This stands in stark contrast to the highly stratified governance systems in Mesopotamia and Egypt, where kings and

pharaohs wielded supreme power.

3. **Absence of Organized Religion**: Unlike Egypt's grand temples and Mesopotamia's ziggurats, more than 100 years of research has shown that the Indus Valley lacks evidence of organized religion. However, the discovery of figurines, particularly of mother goddesses, indicates that they may have celebrated fertility and motherhood. The absence of priestly or religious hierarchies adds another layer to the argument that this civilization had a flatter, more inclusive social structure. However, the presence of figurines, particularly those depicting mother goddesses, suggests that fertility, motherhood, and nature may have played a central role in their spiritual practices. This respect for the natural world and the absence of a formal priestly class point to a potentially flatter, more egalitarian social structure that lacked the rigid hierarchies seen elsewhere.

There is also growing evidence linking the religious practices of the Indus Valley people to early forms of what may later evolve into aspects of Hinduism, particularly animism or nature worship. Excavations of terracotta figurines, seals, and other artifacts suggest a reverence for natural forces, animals, and fertility. The discovery of the "Pashupati" seal, also known as Protoshiva, is especially significant in this regard. This seal features a figure with three faces, seated in a meditative posture, adorned with buffalo horns, and surrounded by animals like the rhinoceros, water buffalo, elephant, and tiger. Some scholars have proposed that this figure may represent an early form of the Hindu god Shiva, particularly in his aspect as the Lord of Beasts (Pashupati). This aligns with the tradition of animism and nature worship, where humans and animals are seen as interconnected and sacred.

Image- Pashupati Seal from Mohenjo-Daro.
Source- Ancient enquiries

Another important seal from Mohenjo-Daro shows the sacred Pipal tree, along with a 'fish' sign and a markhor goat. These images indicate that nature was highly valued, showing how the worship of the natural world was an important part of life in the Indus Valley, highlighting the connection between all living things.

A seal from Mohenjo-daro found by Wheeler in the 1920's. From his 1931 text: "The plant on the [seal] has been identified as a pipal tree, which in India is the Tree of Creation. The arrangement is very conventional and from the lower part of the stem spring two heads similar to those of the so-called unicorn."

Image- Pipal Seal found from Mohenjo-daro
Source- Harappa.com

Thus, the Indus Valley Civilization demonstrated a social model that emphasized communal well-being, gender equality, and collective governance, placing it far ahead of its contemporaries in terms of social advancement.

To wrap things up, the idea of gender equality or even matrilineal structures in the Indus Valley Civilization is still open to interpretation. Some scholars, like Asko Parpola, believe we might be reading too much into the female figurines, suggesting they could symbolize things like fertility or religious beliefs rather than pointing to a matriarchal society. Similarly, Michael Witzel and David Gordon White are a bit skeptical about the evidence supporting the idea of a matrilineal society. They remind us that we need to be careful not to project our modern ideas of gender roles onto ancient civilizations. B.B. Lal also offers an alternative take, saying that these figurines could just as easily represent goddesses or spiritual beings without indicating anything specific about the social structure.

On the flip side, there's Jean-François Jarrige's work from 1991, which shows a more egalitarian society when it comes to gender roles. Unlike other ancient civilizations where women were mostly confined to the home, the Indus Valley seems to have offered them more opportunities. Women were involved in economic activities and even held positions of authority. While there's still a lot we don't know for sure, the evidence points to a society that might have been more progressive and equitable than many of its contemporaries.

# CHAPTER 4

## Vedic Period - The Truly Woke Era

The world never found it strange. The world never found that the creator of life on earth was just subjugated to a second class category , the creator came second to the life it had created. Have you ever known an artist to be second to his art? The world celebrated the creations she made but disturbed, discriminated and oppressed the creator who made this world possible.

But one religion, one set of people always knew that this creator was someone to be respected. That this creator was the one who was to be celebrated for being herself. That was Vedic religion. You can see hundreds of goddesses who have been worshiped since the beginning. As we talked, throughout the stone age as well as the Indus valley civilization people worshiped women and held their status high. Vedic religion in the same manner worshiped women. In fact in its later stage, Hinduism is known to be the only major religion that is driven by the Shakti, the female supreme power. Indians worship women as goddesses because these goddesses are their creators. When the world limited women to being just the child bearers, Vedic people had a different eye to see it. Women were not "only the child bearers", they were "the creators". And I think the generations before us did not think that women were no good because all they could do was just to bear children, they understood that women could do anything and everything because they were capable of doing this, they were capable of creating life. They were seen as similar to the supreme Brahma or the creator of the universe because they could create life. They were worshiped because the fact that a human was capable of doing that, equated women to god itself.

We find many instances from ancient India that tell that women were highly respected beings in society. For example, in Brihaddharma Purana when Maharshi Jabali asks Maharshi Vyasa, "What components are supreme in all three worlds?" Mahrshi Vyasa answers - There is no better location of pilgrimage than the Ganges, no greater world sustainer than Lord Vishnu, no one as venerable as Lord Shiva, and no greater master than one's own mother.

Then Manava Dharma-Sutra also states that motherhood is ten lakh times more important than that of a teacher (upadhyaya, one who gives formal knowledge), a lakh times more important than that of a preceptor (acharya), and a thousand times more important than that of a father.

Musician and Learned Women: 600 B.C.
Palitana Jain Temple (early 11thCentury), Gujarat, India.
Source: National Gallery of Art, Government of India.

In Vedic times, women were even involved in battlegrounds. They used to assist their men in political matters as well. To illustrate, Vispala, lost one leg in the fight and was cured by the Asvins by the addition of an iron leg.

Another example is of Goddess Savita, who played a significant role in the Asvamedha sacrifice. These evidence suggest that women were not only respected as goddesses, but were given a higher status in the society.

Women Horse Riders: Vedic Period.
Kiradu Temple (1153 A.D.-1178 A.D.),
Rajasthan, India.
Source: National Gallery of Art,
Government of India.

We find many examples in our ancient texts that reflect the nature of women's position. One such example is from Manusmriti - Verse 3.56

**"Yatra nāryaśtu pūjyante ramante tatra devatāḥ"**

This verse translates to "Where women are honored, there the gods are pleased."

In Markandeya Purana, the goddess Devi is portrayed as the ultimate reality, and she is equated with Brahman in Durga Saptashati as :

**"Yā devi sarva-bhūteṣu buddhi-rūpeṇa saṁśthitā**

**Namaśtasyai namaśtasyai namaśtasyai namo namaḥ"**

This verse acknowledges the goddess as the one who resides in all beings in the form of intellect (buddhi).

**"Bṛhmātmikā - indicating her identity with the ultimate**

**reality.**

They did not think that women were only good for the household, children and the "chulah and chauka" but they were of the idea that women could do anything because they were able to perform the task that no man could ever do–they could create. But modern society tells us that it is our biggest weakness.

What we see today as shackles, was one of the reasons society revered women. Not because it was a manipulation to tie women to that but because they understood the gravity of this. They knew that without women, the human world would not exist. Our world today dismisses it as a biological disadvantage but think of it, this ability to create life, is it something to be taken for granted? Is it something to be not celebrated? to be not worshiped or to be used to ridicule women, to oppress and be oppressed? Is it something to use as a manipulative tool for making her believe that she can't chase her dreams, because her body will one day cage her?

What if this is the reason to trust her that if nature gave her the ability to do this, if her body is made strong enough to do this, everything else, everything empirical, shall at the very least be doable for her. Women are the exact same goddesses that our religion instituted for, don't take any less of a status that society offers to you, know what your roots say about you.

## The Vedic Feminism

Professor Shashi Prabha Kumar shares some thought-provoking ideas. According to her, Vedic feminism goes beyond what we typically see in modern feminist movements, especially the ones that started in the West. Instead of being aggressive or exclusive, Vedic feminism offers a more balanced and spiritual view, emphasizing equality between men and women in all aspects of life.

Professor Kumar explained that Vedic feminism isn't about one gender being better than the other. It's based on the belief that men and women are equal parts of the Supreme Being, with no distinction on a spiritual level. She highlighted that this principle is deeply rooted in Vedic philosophy, and it's reflected in concepts like **prakriti** (matter) and **purusa** (consciousness) in Samkhya philosophy. These ideas emphasize that both men and women are inseparable and equally necessary.

A powerful symbol of this, Professor Kumar pointed out, is the figure of Ardhanarishvara in Hindu mythology, which represents the inseparable nature of the masculine and feminine energies. This contrasts with many Western and other major religions, where we usually see male gods in the primary role, with female figures often in supporting roles.

Image Ardhanarishvara
Source- Britannica website

In Vedic religion, though, both male and female divine forms are worshiped equally. This stands in contrast to those traditions where the female is often sidelined. Professor Kumar's talk showed how Vedic feminism is inclusive, constructive, and holistic—designed for a truly gender-just society.

Vedic religion however, posed both as equal, ardhanareshwar, one is incomplete without the other.

Look at the vows of Indian marriages, the saptapadi. Prof Kumar said that the equality between men and women is very well explained at the empirical level through the Vedic ritual of marriage, Saptapadi (seven steps). She added that the Vedic marriage ceremony not only signifies equal status of man and woman but also solicits friendship between them.

1. **First Vow (Om esha ekapadi bhava iti prathaman):** The bride and groom vow to nourish each other physically, emotionally, and spiritually. They promise to provide for each other's well-being and happiness.

2. **Second Vow (Om oorje jara dastayaha iti dwitiyam):** The couple promises to develop their physical, mental, and emotional strength to lead a harmonious life together. They vow to overcome obstacles and challenges together.

3. **Third Vow (Om rayas santu joradastayaha iti trutiyam):** The bride and groom pledge to acquire wealth, prosperity, and financial security through righteous means. They commit to managing their resources wisely for the welfare of their family.

4. **Fourth Vow (Om mayo bhavyas jaradastaya ha iti kartavyam):** The couple promises to share each

other's joys and sorrows and to support each other in all circumstances. They vow to uphold their duties and responsibilities towards each other and their families.

5. **Fifth Vow (Om prajabhyaha santu jaradastayaha iti pramanam):** The bride and groom vow to raise a family and fulfill their responsibilities as parents. They promise to nurture and educate their children and to provide them with love, guidance, and support.

6. **Sixth Vow (Om etat rathantaram iti shashtham):** The couple pledges to be faithful and loyal to each other, to trust and respect each other's individuality, and to uphold the sanctity of their marriage vows.

7. **Seventh Vow (Om dhanur vedere iti sapta pade):** In the final vow, the bride and groom affirm their eternal bond of love and companionship. They promise to remain devoted to each other and to cherish their relationship for the rest of their lives.

In her talk, Professor Kumar shed light on a fascinating aspect of Vedic rituals—the crucial role women played in religious ceremonies. She mentioned that men couldn't perform yajnas (sacred rituals) without their wives beside them. In fact, it was believed that the presence of the wife was essential for the proper performance of these rites.

To explain this further, Professor Kumar brought up an interesting point from the Brahmana texts, where husbands would refer to their wives using three special terms. The first was Jaya, meaning the divine lady who bears his children. The second term was Jani, referring to the wife as the mother. And finally, Patni, which means legally wedded wife, a term that carries great significance because it is directly linked to Dharma. When a man addresses his wife as **Dharma Patni**, he's acknowledging her as not only his legally wedded wife but also someone who shares his duties, responsibilities, and spiritual journey, said Professor Kumar.

She also highlighted an important teaching from the Atharva Veda—that no religious action could be performed by the husband without his wife sitting by his side. To illustrate this point, she mentioned the famous example from the **Ramayana**, where Lord Ram needed to perform a yajna. Since Sita was not with him at the time, he couldn't complete the ritual. So, to fulfill the requirement, Lord Ram placed a golden murti (idol) of Sita by his side, symbolizing the necessity of the wife's presence in these sacred ceremonies.

Interestingly, Professor Kumar noted that women, on the other hand, were not always bound by the same rules. In many cases, women could perform specific rites on their own, even without their husbands. This emphasizes the spiritual independence women had during the Vedic times.

She also spoke about the **Rishikas**, the female seers in the Vedas who had realized mantras, just like their male counterparts. There were over 28 **Rishikas** mentioned in the Vedic hymns, and some of the most notable among them included Suryaa, Apala, Atreyi, Vishvavara, Shachi, and Indrani. Along with these female seers, Professor Kumar pointed out the many powerful female deities present in the Vedas, such as Saraswati, Usha, Aditi, and Kuhu.

This really shows that women during the Vedic period were not confined to just the home or household duties. In fact, they were encouraged to step out and actively participate in intellectual discussions and debates. According to

Professor Kumar, women were allowed and even expected to go to the **Sabha** (assembly) and contribute to discussions. They were recognized as intellectually accomplished partners in these conversations.

Professor Kumar also addressed a misconception about how women were viewed in the Vedas. She emphasized that the term **Abala nari**—meaning "weak woman"—is never used in the Vedas. Instead, women were referred to as **Aditi**, which literally means "independent" or "one who is not dependent on anyone." When people invoked the deity Aditi, they were calling upon the form of womanhood that embodied independence and strength.

In fact, Professor Kumar shared that, in certain places within the Vedic texts, it's even said that women were sometimes seen as being more spiritually accomplished than men. This reflects a complete and complementary relationship between men and women in Vedic culture. Women weren't merely silent observers—they played an active role in both the household and the spiritual world. And we need to understand this in the context of that time period. Vedic age predominantly laid emphasis on spiritual growth and it was the ultimate goal of human life. So, when we talk about the accomplishments of women during this time, their mention in the Vedic texts, shows that their participation in this period was significant. When we see the life of women during that time, let us understand that the aspects that were important during that time were very different from the age we are living in right now and we need to keep the context in mind always.

Now besides spirituality let's talk about the main occupations of women in vedic age.

- Agriculture
- Animal Husbandry

- Weaving and Spinning
- Metalworking
- Trading and Commerce
- Religious Functions
- Governance and Administration
- Craftsmanship
- Healing and Medicine
- Education and Learning

During her talk, Professor Kumar highlighted the remarkable role women played in Vedic society, mentioning that women weren't just confined to their homes but actively contributed to various aspects of society. She explained that according to the Vedas, women worked in many fields, ranging from labor to scholarship. They weren't just limited to one role—in fact, they were Acharayas, or teachers.

Beyond formal teaching, women also played the crucial role of being the first educators for their children. They were responsible for passing on samskaras, which are the cultural values and teachings that shape character and prepare an individual for life's main objectives, such as liberation, making a living, forming character, and preserving culture. In Vedic thought, these samskaras were considered essential for living a meaningful life, and women had a key role in instilling these values from the very beginning.

Professor Kumar also touched upon another significant role women held in Vedic society—physicians. Women were not only caregivers within their homes but also healers in their communities. She mentioned the sayings of Shachi Indrani, who demonstrated that women were also great orators, showcasing their intellectual presence and communication skills in society.

What's particularly interesting is that women during the Vedic period were often seers and celibates too, known as Brahmacharinis. They were deeply involved in spiritual practices, and many of them are even mentioned in the Vedic texts as powerful figures. The Vedas include many female deities that were worshiped, and these goddesses played a vital role in Vedic religion and rituals.

Women's roles went beyond just intellectual or religious pursuits, though. Professor Kumar emphasized that women not only cared for their families but also took responsibility for looking after animals and the environment. They were seen as vital to nurturing not only their homes but society at large. Women were regarded as the empress or true owner of the household, and this position came with significant rights and opportunities.

In terms of their economic contribution, women were highly skilled in various forms of craftsmanship. They were involved in weaving cloth, spinning thread, and even making pottery, baskets, and jewelry—both for household use and for trade. Women played an essential role in producing items that contributed to the family's livelihood and the broader community's economy.

One of the most striking things Professor Kumar mentioned was the level of education women attained during the Vedic period. Many women were scholars, well-versed in sacred texts, including the Vedas. They weren't just learning these texts—they actively composed hymns and were involved in music and dance. Even women from lower social strata took part in skilled trades like spinning, weaving, and needlework.

Interestingly, the educators of the Vedic period had divided women into two distinct groups when it came to education. The first group, called Brahmavadini, were lifelong students of philosophy and theology, dedicated to their studies for their entire lives. The second group, Sadyodvahas, continued their education until they married, typically at the age of 15 or 16. Despite their different paths, both groups had access to the same educational opportunities, allowing women to contribute to society in intellectual and spiritual ways.

Many educated women became teachers, or Upadhyayinis, sharing their knowledge with others. There were also women poets and philosophers during this time. The Vedic period saw many capable and wise women, like Apala, Ghosha, and Visvavara, who not only composed mantras but were considered to be of the same rank as rishis (sages). They were recognized for their intelligence and spiritual insight.

Professor Kumar also mentioned Lopamudra, one of the most well-known female preachers of the Vedic period. She is believed to have composed and preached as many as 179 hymns of the first book of the Rig Veda, alongside her husband, Sage Agastya. Lopamudra's contributions highlight the fact that women were not only educated but also made lasting contributions to religious and spiritual life.

## Some Instances From Vedas And Related Texts.

**"O scholarly woman, the way a river breaks away mightiest of hills and rocks, the scholarly woman destroys myths and hypes through her intellect alone. May we bow to women through our polite words and noble actions." — Rigveda 6.61.2**

**"A scholarly woman, the entire life of society depends upon you. You provide us with the right knowledge. May you bring knowledge to all segments of society." — Rigveda 2.41.17**

**"Parents should gift their daughter intellectuality and power of knowledge when she leaves for the husband's home. They should give her a dowry of knowledge." — Rig 10.85.7**

**"O wife! Become the queen and manager of everyone in the family of your husband." — Atharva 14.1.20**

**"O bride! You shall bring bliss to all and direct our homes towards our purpose of living." — Atharva 14.1.61**

**"O wife! I am knowledgeable and you are also knowledgeable. If I am Samved then you are Rigved." — Atharva 14.2.71**

In the Brihadaranyaka Upanishad, people bear their mother's name with them as she played an important role in shaping their early development.

The teaching of Hinduism is same for both sexes and all have to follow the karma, ahinsa and for others. In Chandogya Upanishad, women were regarded. They had the right to wear yajnopavita and entitled for upnayan sanskar. According to the Gobhila Grhya Sutra and Kathaka Grhya Sutra, they used to utter vedic mantras. In smriti shastra, it may be mentioned that the word 'patni' implies equal participation of men and women in sacrifices.

If a woman decided to live freely, she had the right to live alone. The practice of single parenting and unwed motherhood could be seen in ancient India, although not very favored. There was a provision of punishment for the men and women in case of cheating with their spouses, signifying gender equality.

## Abortions And Contraceptives In This Age

Abortion was a sin, but contraceptive methods were in vogue. A mechanical device made of stone, artificially induced changes to make the vaginal cavity rough or dry, herbal and herbo-mineral contraceptive preparations for local and oral use by men and women along with breathing exercises mentioned in the Brihadaranyaka Upanishad were among the earliest mention methods to prevent conception.

The mention of contraceptive methods, even in ancient texts, suggests that women and men sought ways to control fertility, indicating a desire for some level of autonomy in family planning.

The availability and use of contraceptive methods, even in early times, may have provided women with some degree of control over their reproductive destinies, challenging traditional patriarchal structures where women's roles were often limited to childbearing and caregiving.

The condemnation of abortion while accepting contraceptive methods may also reflect broader social norms and expectations surrounding sexuality, reproduction, and gender roles. Abortion may be viewed as more socially disruptive or morally objectionable due to its association with the termination of potential life, while contraception is seen as a means of responsible family planning.

# CHAPTER 5
## The Axis Of Hinduism

A week into the research for this chapter, I was mind boggled with the amount of information that exists on the "Hindu religion". I didn't know how I could search through each and everything available on the subject and go through every purana, every shastra, every book that exists out there, to understand what they said about women, more so I don't know sanskrit, so all I can rely upon are the translations. I felt demotivated and it broke me because every other text I read had some good things and then a load of negative positions on women. I thought to myself that maybe the purpose of my book is wrong, there is nothing or maybe heartbreakingly just a little good in my culture that I can use to share with my readers. However, a day after that, I was searching on the internet hopping onto the last hope to continue on this path, and this is when I found an almost hitting statement. It was said by Acharya Prashant, who is an advocate of the vedanta darshana. He said, to understand Hinduism, or what we call Sanatan Dharma, Upanishads can be taken as a reference text as they are the revered extensions of Vedas, and Upanishads remove the entire basis of difference between us all.

I was shocked to know this. "There are smaller traditions and greater traditions and vedas and Upanishads represent the greater traditions of what we call Hinduism, according to him. Every time you stand at a contradiction, you must refer to these greater literary traditions, as he said, "Who all will you listen to, "kis kis ki baatein maante rahoge, pick the centers?"

Sonaturally I wantedtounderstandthe UPANISHADS.

Farzaneh Azamlotf is a researcher from Iran, who studied the vedanta and he says "Upanishad is a quest for truth, and seeks it from the path of logic and rationality." This is what intrigued me too. He further says that within the structure of Hindu sacred literature, the Upanishads are regarded as extensions of the "Aranyakas," delving deeper into contemplative insights. Aranyakas are called the forest books. The writers of Aranyakas are known as "Caviya Satiya Sarvata," wise individuals who lived and meditated in deep untouched and dense forests of India, dedicating their lives to knowing their own selves. These same sages are said to have later created the Upanishads.

Upanishads are based on the more refined and understood mystical experiences of these sages, which are believed to be received from a higher divine source. They conveyed that these revelations often embodied the concept of Unity of Existence, transferred through hidden, dense and symbolic ideas. Firstly, they were written as Aranyakas and then the transition from the Aranyakas to Upanishads marked a unique chapter of spiritual learning and self-discovery, a phase that concluded with the philosophical maturity found in the Upanishads.

Max Müller posits that the Upanishads were originally oral teachings, passed intimately from master to disciple, and have profoundly influenced not only Hinduism but also Buddhism. At their core, these texts explore themes of spirituality, self-purification, and the eternal truth that permeated ancient Indian thought—a distinctive path to understanding the self and the cosmos.

Great reformists like Raja Ram Mohan Roy had also rejected mainstream religious practices, instead embracing the Upanishadic concept of God as an impersonal, absolute power. Drawing from these teachings, he challenged orthodox Hindus who saw a personal god as essential to their faith. Following in his path, Dayananda Saraswati

(1824-1883) also established the **Arya Samaj** reform movement in 1875. This movement confronted the Indian caste system, promoting the equality of all people based on self-knowledge and the pursuit of truth. It emphasized that social status should be determined not by birth but by one's actions, or **Karam** (virtuous deeds).

As people of everyday lives we just know the stories, the anecdotes of the secondary and tertiary texts, we ourselves don't know the core of our religion. We all just know what we have heard through someone or somewhere, none of us know the primary words of the pioneers. I still can't get you the primary research as I don't know Sanskrit and I don't have access to the original texts and manuscripts. But I realized that I can at least bring out a different perspective, a perspective that can help us challenge the status quo. Hinduism is not one philosophy, not one doctrine, there are many schools of thought, many philosophies, many sages and many manuscripts. Going through everything was obviously not possible for me, but out of everything that I researched, I personally really enjoyed learning about Vedanta philosophy.

Vedanta means, where vedas end too. This arm comprises 108 Upanishads that are known to have survived. The reason that I liked this philosophy was because it removes the basis of every discrimination that exists in today's world. One line that stuck with me was, Upanishads, question the existence, **you are not your body, not your mind, then who are you?** And they state that every person is the same at the spiritual level. It states, "Aham Brahmasmi", "mai hi Brahma hun". And this is not some egotistical claim, in my understanding, it means that "I am everything and nothing at the same time, I am everything that exists and will exist at the same time, we are all the same, we are Brahma."

See, now I am not an expert at historical texts, but as a common reader, I just wanted to bring this philosophy out. I wanted to add that there are different schools of thought and this one interpretation in Vedanga actually could provide a good basis to understand till what level have people questioned existence and everything that comes along with it, discrimination, oppression, everything.

Let me now take you to a story from Upanishads.

Within the revered texts of the Upanishads, there are glimpses of women who defied limitations and sought something greater in their lives.

One such woman was Maitreyi, the wife of the sage Yajnavalkya. As Yajnavalkya approached the end of his life—or, in some versions, considered becoming a wandering ascetic—he decided to settle matters concerning his two wives. He intended to provide them with financial security for their future.

Yajnavalkya assessed his wives with a distinct lens. Maitreyi was described as someone deeply engaged in philosophical discussions, while Katyayani was seen as more focused on traditional, domestic concerns. Maitreyi, however, was not content with mere material wealth. She had a deeper, more profound aspiration. When Yajnavalkya offered her a substantial financial settlement, Maitreyi questioned the value of such wealth. She wondered if possessing all the riches in the world would grant her immortality. Yajnavalkya explained that wealth alone could not bestow immortality; it merely allowed one to live a comfortable life.

Her query was more than a rhetorical question; it was a profound inquiry into the nature of existence and the pursuit of higher knowledge. Maitreyi was aware that true immortality lay not in material possessions but in the understanding of deeper truths.

Yajnavalkya responded to her quest with a deep philosophical explanation. He spoke of the ultimate self, or Atman, suggesting that all things cherished are ultimately reflections of this self. To understand this self was to grasp the essence of immortality.

In their conversation, Maitreyi's pursuit of spiritual wisdom over material gain was clear. She sought a deeper truth, one that transcended the conventional roles assigned to her. This intellectual and spiritual curiosity placed her alongside other notable women of the time, such as Gargi, who engaged in profound philosophical debates.

Now the question is how the Hindus, who believe in dualism, have accepted unity of the creator of the universe.

## What Do We Understand From This?

This story reminds us that the core of our religion has always been rooted in the search for a higher truth. At its essence, it goes beyond the distinctions we often get caught up in—those of body, mind, and the physical world we live in. The real truth lies in the understanding that the **Atman**—the soul—has no gender, no caste, and no divisions. It's this soul, shared by all, that makes everyone fundamentally equal.

The focus, as Professor Kumar pointed out, is on raising one's chetna, or consciousness. The people who deserve recognition and a higher status in society aren't the ones born into a particular gender, family, or social group. It's those who strive to elevate their consciousness, their awareness, who truly stand out.

Interestingly, this idea of ranking doesn't only apply to humans; it also applies to the gods and goddesses in Hinduism. There are two kinds of energies, or **Shaktis**: **apara shakti** and **para shakti**. **Apara shakti** represents the lower, more physical aspects of energy, tied to the dualistic nature of the world—feminine and masculine, light and dark. This is the realm of **dvaita**, or dualism. On the other hand, **para shakti** is the higher, non-dual energy, which reflects the idea of **advaita**—that everything and everyone stems from the same, singular source, without any distinctions or separations.

This brings us to one of the greatest sources of confusion in religion: the concept of assigning gender to the divine. **Shakti** is often assigned a feminine gender and contrasted with **Shiva**, who is seen as masculine. Similarly, **Purusha** is thought of as male, and **Prakriti** as female. But here's the problem—these are human concepts. The only reference point we have for gender is the one we've been conditioned to understand in our world, and we project that onto the divine.

But what if we took a step back and stripped away all these highly charged gender labels when we describe the divine? Let's look at it from the perspective of **Shaktism**, the tradition from which the fierce, feminist goddess Kali comes. In **Shaktism**, the ultimate reality is referred to as **Brahma**—the source of everything—which is both with form and without form, both present in this world and beyond it.

The transcendent part of this ultimate reality is beyond our universe and is formless. It doesn't have attributes like name, shape, space, or time. However, the immanent aspect of the divine does have form—it's everything we see and experience in the world around us. So, how do we understand these two aspects? One way is to call them **Shiva** and **Shakti**.

**Shiva** represents the transcendent, formless aspect of reality, while **Shakti** represents the form, the creative force that brings everything into being. But here's the thing: **Shiva** isn't inherently masculine, and **Shakti** isn't inherently feminine. These labels of male and female come from our own learned ideas about what it means to be a man or a woman.

We call **Shakti** feminine because she represents the creative power of the divine, and in most species, females are the ones who carry the creative, reproductive power. But this doesn't mean she has the characteristics of a human woman, just like **Shiva** doesn't have the characteristics of a human man. Instead, it's much more helpful to think of **Shiva** and **Shakti** as formless and with form. They're two sides of the same reality—one can't exist without the other.

Although they seem separate, it's impossible to draw a clear line between where **Shiva** ends and **Shakti** begins. **Shakti** is **Shiva** in motion, while **Shiva** is **Shakti** in stillness. They are inseparable, and together, they represent the complete cycle of existence, creation, and transformation. So rather than getting caught up in gender distinctions, we can think of the divine as an interplay of energy—motion and stillness, form and formlessness—all working together as one.

The highest power in Hinduism therefore, the Brahma, is not a male. Rather Brahma has no gender. The highest power, the highest god is formless, un-gendered, undivided, there is no 'he' or 'she'. The highest power is equality.

In a very famous verse of the Devi Mahatmyam, Shakti is revered thus:

**namo devyai mahādevyai śivāyai satataṃ namaḥ।**
**namaḥ prakṛtyai bhadrāyai niyatāḥ praṇatāḥ smatāṃ**

"We bow to the Goddess, the Great Goddess, who is Shiva, the eternal. We bow to the Goddess who is Nature, who is auspicious and eternal. To her, we bow reverentially."

Shiva is formless. Shakti is form. As Nature, Shakti is all forms. As in everything in the cosmos:

- Tamas, rajas, and sattva.
- Stars, planets, and moons.
- Galaxies, black holes, and dark matter.
- Light, energy, and matter.
- Electrons, neutrons, and protons.
- Quarks, leptons, and bosons.
- Earthquakes, tsunamis, and thunderstorms.
- Breath, mind, and body.
- DNA, chromosomes, and genes.
- Hormones, cellular reactions, and neural pathways.
- Viruses, bacteria, and parasites.
- Good and evil.
- Male and female.
- Misogyny and misandry.
- Justice and injustice.

You get the point. There's nothing in the universe that is not Shakti. Whether the exploitation is that by men of women, women of women, or women of men is really irrelevant. Remember, Shakti is both man and woman. How much the said man or woman is deluded is the primary drive for exploitation.

So, our religion actually removes all the basis of discrimination. It's not just the gender aspect, our highest texts tell us that since you are not the mind, not the body, we are all equal at a spiritual level. We are all manifestations of Shakti therefore **only delusions lead to exploitation**, the truth only leads to equality. The core of Hinduism or Sanatan dharam can never sanction discrimination. It might be the interpretations of these texts that have caused problems but a religion that removes the entire basis of inequality, how can it teach to discriminate, to exploit, to oppress?

So, next time if someone quotes a scripture justifying the discriminatory practices, please remind them and yourself that our religion strips off all the basis of this from our existence. It teaches us to rise above it not get entangled with the manipulation of the mind, of the duality, of the maya. And even though these might seem like far away concepts from reality but if we look closer we might actually see that this is the only realm where we can actually find grounds for equality, we can find grounds to rise above every difference.

# CHAPTER 6

## Reimagining Women from Ancient India

Our mythology is infused with powerful female figures and goddesses, inherently containing feminist elements that have been distorted over time. By reinterpreting these stories, we seek to restore the original empowerment of these figures, offering a fresh perspective that aligns with contemporary feminist values.

## Draupadi

In a world where women were shadows of the men and restrictions surrounded their lives, from the sacred flames emerged Draupadi. Her face with the fervor of a thousand suns; she was a fierce soul who came into the world to lead.

Her name translated to 'Daughter of Dhrupad' but her destiny held a different personality for her. A curious kid since the beginning, she would repeatedly ask about the story of her birth. Her Dhai Ma, her caretaker, would surrender to the sparkles and fire in her eyes, narrating to her how she grew out of the flames. From the sacred flames that Draupadi had emerged from had prophesied her 'role in the future'. This was a mystery for Draupadi; she wanted to solve it. "How am I going to play a role in the future? Am I meant for something extraordinary?" she used to ask herself.

Growing up, she was a rebel. Finding her own way to hunt for answers, she would take steps alien to the princess's life. For instance, in her teenage years, she wanted to move freely in the kingdom. King Dhrupad, who had asked for a prince, got princess Draupadi by the wholly fire. Therefore Dhrupad resented her and she was not allowed to do much. Her actions to see the world beyond her constraints could have landed her in soup. Despite knowing the results, she disguised herself and left the royal palace with Dhai Ma. She was an unstoppable spirit, a perfect balance of witty and clever.

She was never a bonded bird. Frustrated by the barren environment liked by her father, she was more a cheerful one. Even in the royal palace with gray marbles, she used to manifest her very own palace with flowers and trees. She was the seeker for solutions. Being born with dark skin, she learned the art of staying confident in her own skin and aced it too. In a world where 'how to become a perfect wife' was a hot topic for women, she was more inclined towards the study of administration, diplomacy, and war. To fulfill her desire, she even began taking lectures with her brother. She was just a student but had a deeper understanding of the difference between right and wrong. On an occasion mentioned in the book The Palace of Illusions, when the brahmin priest mentioned women as the 'root cause of problem' she intervened. Knowing that could lead to her dismissal from the rest of the classes, she proceeds to speak her thoughts out. She was barred from the classes, but she managed to learn from the books her brother was being referred to. Such was her determination. Amid all her teenage life, she was eager to know her real self and her role in crafting the future.

Draupadi was not someone who was to bow against the customary laws. We find a conversation between her and Dhai Ma where she was being taught how to respect the more loved queen of the king. This practice was to make her a 'perfect wife' in the future. "I don't need to learn that!" she protested. "My husband won't take another wife—I'll make him promise that before I marry him!". These lines express her thoughts. How she was a charming personality questioning the status quo.

Being raised in a royal household, she felt the ignorance

that surrounded her. She wanted to see the kingdom and was a good observer as well. This helped her understand the happenings in her surroundings.

When Shikhandi, her long-lost sister, came back to Panchal kingdom, everyone was terrified. Even King Dhrupad and Prince Drishyadyum were concerned. Draupadi, on the other hand, was excited. The news of her sister, whom she didn't know existed, made her curious to know her story.

She was not meant to fit in; she was made to stand out. Even the decision of Gandhari to blindfold herself made no sense to Draupadi. "If my husband couldn't see, I'd make doubly sure to keep my own eyes open so that I could report everything that was going on to him." Such were the thoughts of Draupadi. She wasn't a puppet; she was an independent soul.

As she grew up, she got married to the Pandavas. She was ridiculed and humiliated for polyandry but she never bowed down to the insults. On being lost in the game of dice to the Kauravas, it was she who stood up for her own dignity. In the assembly where no man had the courage to question the wrong, her eyes filled with fire made everyone ashamed of their silence. It was she who took the vow of avenging her own fate and not tying her hair until justice was served. This humiliation transformed her into a powerful symbol of resistance. It was not only for her that she fought for; it was for all those women who had been silenced. "This battle is not for land; it is for honor—our honor!". Her words were wrapped in courage; she guided the war not for victory but for justice.

As the war loomed over the land of Kurukshetra, Draupadi became a war cry. She guided the warriors, reminding them of what was on the stake. When finally the dust settled on the battlefield, she envisioned a world where the voices of women were heard and where justice was served.

Thus, Draupadi was not a woman shaped by her circumstances but by her own narratives. She is an embodiment of strength and has been inspiring women of all generations. She has proved to be a symbol of feminine power, the one filled with fire and storms. She was a firebrand who lit the way for generations to come.

## Ganga

The ancient land of India has been home to many holy rivers. The sacred water flows like veins through the channels crafted by these mighty rivers over time. Ganga, one of the most pious rivers, stands out more than just a river; it is revered as "Ganga Ma." She is a living entity, an embodiment of maternal strength and purity. Originating from the Northern Heights, she sprawls the plains as she moves, forming one of the largest plains in the world—the Gangetic-plains. Ever since the beginning of civilization, she has been serving as a source of life, providing water to the inhabitants. Her aura carries warmth, accepting and attracting people of all faiths. She is the one promising redemption and liberation. A dip in her lap is seen to cut the cord between births and deaths; it liberates the devotees from the shackles of karma.

But beneath this soft maternal aura lies a fierce energy. It is the force that has been shaping the legendary stories, the mythological epics, and the cosmic realms. As per Hindu mythology, Ganga is more than a river. She has been seen as a devoted daughter, a dedicated mother, and a lover. She is the daughter of King Himavan and Queen Menavati. She is the sister of Mata Parvati and holds descent from the lineage of devotion. She has been seen as an energy that carries the potential to purify the souls. Her aura is so magnificent that it can wash away the sins. But she is more than an embodiment of purity; she is a force that couldn't be confined. She is a force that flows with purpose—the force that knows no bounds.

Lord Vishnu has described the importance of Ganga, saying to Garuda, the eagle God, his divine vahana:

**"Darshana Tsparshanatpanattatha Gangeti Keertanat Punatyapunyanpurushana Shatashotha Sahasrashah"**

Meaning: "Thousands of man's sins get destroyed by the holy sight of the Ganges, and he becomes pure by the touch of the water of Ganges, by consuming it, or just by pronouncing"

In the Hindu mythology, we have many tales illustrating Ganga as the fierce force. One such tale is of King Bhagiratha.

King Bhagiratha was the son of King Dilipa. He was dedicated to please Lord Vishnu—a task that couldn't be fulfilled by his ancestors. He was to liberate the ashes of his ancestors, who were stuck in the realm due to the curse of Sage Kapila. His continuous appeasement and penance made Lord Vishu appear in front of him. He put forth his wish and asked Lord Brahma for his blessings to help him. Brahma knew that the liberation of the ashes would be done by Ganga only. But he was also aware of her overwhelming power and her fierceness. Not just him; even the gods knew the devastation that could take place if Ganga was allowed to fulfil his wish. But King Bhagiratha was desperate. He prayed to Lord Shiva, who agreed to guide Ganga safely on Earth. Even Lord Shiva was aware of the immense energy that Ganga carried, and he captured the force of Ganga in his matted hair. When he released it in a balanced manner, even that wasn't enough. The mighty Ganga burst forth and flooded the hermitage of Sage Janhu. It was he who recognized her as his daughter and named her Jahnavi.

It reflects that Ganga was seen as a source of immense power. She has always known her purpose. When she walked down from heaven, she was well aware of herself and her duties. She was a destined force to play a pivotal role in Mahabharata. In her marriage with King Shantnau, she made a profound vow, which was an example of her fierce independence. She asked the King of Hastinapur never to question her actions. This promise that she asked for was a declaration of autonomy; it was a plot to fulfil her promise of liberation to the eight Vasus. She was the force that was destined to free them from the curse of Sage Vashistha. It shows that a force like Ganga could even undo the curses of mighty sages such was her strength. Ganga was the architect of her own destiny. She was moving with an aim, a clear focus. Her decisions were to protect the cosmic order.

Even in today's time, we refer to Ganga as 'mata' or 'ma'. She is seen as a nurturing force, a fierce energy. In the Mahabharata, she gave birth to the epitome of virtue and raised the greatest warrior, Bhishma. She raised him as a man of morals. His values were so that he gave the throne of the kingdom for the happiness of his father. He was the one navigating the kingdom of Hastinapur through the turbulent waters. But Ganga anchored him. Being a mother, she constantly reminded him of his purpose. It was her influence that guided Bhishma through gusty winds. It was her spirit that made him face all the odds with utmost courage.

Apart from the mythological mentions, we find the stories of her sacred currents in later times also. When Ganga finally assumed the form of a river, she was recognized as a liberating force of all beings. It shows that women icons were shown to be fierce yet soft, liberating and devastating at the same time, they were not the abala naris. One compelling incident is of King Didinga. He was the ruler of the Ganga Dynasty and thereby claimed his descent from the solar dynasty. In the battle of Vaimbalguri, he was fighting against the force of the Rashtrakuta kingdom. During the war, he got severely wounded. He anticipated his death, and using a knife, he chopped his arm off. He then asked a messenger to take it and submerge it in the current of Ganga. Even at the time of his death, he wanted to secure the blessing of Ganga. Everybody bowed down to her.

This was the profoundness of the force. Even at the time of his mortality, King Didinga knew that only the divine feminine power could bless him with liberation. And this is important to know that liberation is considered the most important goal of human life in Hinduism and on the earth, Ganga, a woman has the power to grant it.

Even in today's world, we see Ganga as a potent power. The one who carries the door of liberation. She is seen as the absolute knowledge; a knowledge so deep that it can purify the souls. She is fierce and stormy. She is calm and free. She is unboundable, and her currents speak liberation. Her story is a testament to the power of femininity.

In the end, I would like to quote the words from the Bhagavad Gita:

Lord Krishna declares when imparting the highest spiritual knowledge to Arjuna:

"Of purifiers I am the wind, of the wielders of weapons I am Rama, of fish I am the shark, and of flowing rivers I am the Ganga."

## Satyavati

The Mahabharata as an epic has given us the holy verses of the Bhagavad Gita. It has made us understand the realities of this life through its various characters. If I say Mahabharata, your brain will quickly respond with towering names like Bhishma, Kauravas, Pandavas, Kunti, Ganga, Dhritarashtra, and Draupadi. But let's pause for a moment and look at another important feminine figure who didn't receive much light. She wasn't just a beautiful face; she had a brilliant mind. A curious spirit with the zeal to find her answers. She was the woman determined to guide her own journey by crafting her own path. She was Satyavati, a fisherman's daughter who became the Kuru Queen.

To many of us, Satyavati has been portrayed as a queen who was gripped by the sorrows of an empty throne; as a queen who had sown the seeds of war because of her decisions. But Satyavati was more than that. She was a fierce lady in the male-dominated world. A strong soul who knew her aim. Parts of her early life, when she shared her time with Rishi Parashar, were not her nature. It was a guided instinct to sail her own boat and to craft her own fate.

She was the daughter of Dasharaj, a fisherman. Though not his biological daughter, he left no stone unturned to love her like her own blood. In reality, she was his niece. Her story was a tragedy that was wrapped by the blanket of love by Dasharaja. As a kid, she had no idea who her mother was. When she was young, she used to ask about her parents from Dasharaja, who would tell her a mythological story about her existence. She would listen to all his tales wide-eyed, but the fire within her demanding the truth kept burning. As she was growing up, she wanted to dig deeper into the history of her existence and her lineage.

One day, she confronted Dasharaja. She sat down in front of her father, with eyes sparkling with determination. She wasn't ready to listen to the same story; she demanded the truth. Her curiosity and energy were such that Dasharaja had to unfold the chapters from her past. He unveiled her true parentage: she was the daughter of King Chedi. Gathering the courage, Dasharaj told her that she was a victim of an unforgivable crime. Her curiosity peaked, and she was not ready to hold back. "You are the daughter of Adrika," told Dasharaj. He followed the declaration by unveiling that Adrika was her sister who was sexually assaulted by Uparichar Vasu, the king of Chedi. Listening to this, her anger surged. She had faced the reality that was hiding under the mythological story of her existence. But Satyavati, instead of succumbing to despair, made a vow, "I will not be a wretched victim like her."

Satyavati was a focused woman. She always knew what she wanted. She was smart and strategic. Her curiosity made her question things, and this habit evolved as a quality of understanding things in a better manner. Take, for example, the instance when Rishi Parashar paid her father a visit. As per the conversation mentioned in the book 'The Fisher Queen's Dynasty' by Kavita Kane, on being asked certain questions by the Rishi, Satyavati answered them all. Her answer reflected her awareness about the surroundings and her presence of mind. Rishi Parashar replied, "You seem to know your politics well from such a young age." "I am fifteen," she shot back, "young enough to experience it and old enough to realize it." This reflects the sharpness of her brian. She was an active observer from a very young age. Being a woman with perspective, she understood her world and how to navigate it.

Being an extraordinary woman, Satyavati had the courage to choose her own path in an era where women were eclipsed under the directions of men. Being a calculative woman, she made her decisions after estimating the consequences. She used to think ten steps ahead before taking any action. For instance, when Satyavati was alone in the boat with Rishi Parashar, she could sense the underlying desires in Rishi's gaze. She understood the situation and the possible outcomes. As a result, she didn't hesitate to ask Rishi about the future of the child if she conceived. She was aware of society and the consequences too. She initiated the conversation to solve problems that could arise in the future. Therefore, we can conclude that Satyavati had strong decision-making potential.

Satyavati was aware of her powers as a woman. After her association with Rishi Parashar, she told Dasharaj, her father, "'I—not Fate or God—shall be responsible for my own happiness, my own future. I promise myself, I will not be the victim anymore, nor will my child. His father is famous and respected, so let him live with him. He will gain more respect there than with an unwed fisherwoman." Her words indicate her fierceness and independence. She wasn't a puppet. She was the sailor of her own boat. She knew what she wanted, and she didn't hesitate to take steps in that direction. She kept her motherly instincts aside and decided to let her baby be with Rishi Parashar. Later, when she met her son, she didn't hesitate, even a little, to accept him as her own. This is the instance from a time when unmarried mothers were seen as a stigma in society. Unlike Kunti, who cast away her son Karan out of fear of society,

Satyavati embraced her son with pride. But she had the courage to let him go as well. She wanted her son to rise up to a respected level in society. She knew it was possible when he lived with his father, Rishi Parashar. This explains the nature of Satyavati, a fearless but well-calculated woman.

Satyavati was not just a mother; she was a woman with ambition. She wanted to become a powerful woman. She was the one who created her own destiny. So when King Shantanu crossed her path, she recognized the chance to rewrite her fate. She saw it as a possibility to become the Kuru Queen. In the words of Kussum Choppara, an author, "If you consider the Mahabharata as a political drama, Satyavati comes across as the most politically sharp person, whose sway on the other characters and the events to come is far-reaching."

Satyavati didn't want to live only as a fisherman's daughter. She aspired to become a woman of higher class. King Shantanu was attracted towards Satyavati. Knowing that he had an eye on her, she proposed to be with him only if he accepted her as the queen. She didn't stop here. She had far-sight. Knowing about Gangaputra Bhishma, she made a bold statement, but under the veil of her father. Dasharaj proposed his grandchild to be the official heir of the throne. This was the moment that weaved the story of the Mahabharata. It was from here, from the desires of Satyavati, that the stage for the Mahabharata was set. Her decision was the seed for intra family disputes, which would rise further. The political smartness of Satyavati and her undaunted spirit, who seeked freedom and growth, was evident here.

Satyavati had her own plans and her own ways. Yet, the universe has a way of challenging our aspirations. Despite becoming the queen, her desire to see her lineage thriving looked only like a dream. She had lost both her sons and her husband, King Shantanu. It was her and the two widows of her sons to rule the empire. But her spirit was unbroken.

Satyavati called upon Rishi Veda Vyasa, her son from Rishi Parashar. Yes, you read the name right. Rishi Veda Vyasa, you would later write the Mahabharata. She urged him to bless her with grandchildren with the widows of her late sons. As a result, the Kuru kingdom saw the faces of Pandu, Dhritarashtra, and Vidur. It was here that the ripples of war and drama were created in the Mahabharata.

From being a fisherman's daughter, who had not even known her parents when a child, Satyavati grew up to become the Queen of Hastinapur. She wasn't only a character of the Mahabharata; she was an architect. Her choices and decisions laid the foundation stones for the upcoming future of the Kuru empire and its existence.

She was a fearless soul, a woman who knew her desires. Her dedication to achieve what she wanted led her to a solution-oriented mindset. It was her experiences and sharpness of mind that made her emerge as an extraordinary woman of those times. Her legacy? A reminder that true power lies in taking a stand for yourself and creating your own destiny.

## Kali

**I found this story to be one of my favorites.**

The story of Kali begins with Shiva, the great ascetic and the embodiment of balance, urging Maa Parvati to discover the hidden force within her—the force of Kali. Parvati, who is often revered for her grace, patience, and nurturing qualities, was also the vessel of a far more potent and untamed power, one that even Shiva acknowledged was beyond his control. He knew that in the depths of her being, lay Kali, the fierce goddess of destruction and transformation.

Shiva, understanding the challenges that lay ahead, encouraged Parvati to embrace this aspect of herself, not as a departure from her identity but as a fuller realization of it. He guided her to tap into the raw, primal energy that resides within every woman—the energy that is often feared, misunderstood, and suppressed. As Parvati delved deeper into her own consciousness, she began to shed the layers of cultural expectations and constraints that had long defined her.

Emerging from this inner journey was Kali, the quintessential embodiment of shakti, the female power. She was not just another goddess but a force of nature, unrestrained by the bounds of societal norms or the gaze of those who sought to contain her. Kali, with her wild hair, dark skin, and fierce demeanor, represented the culmination of all that is raw, untamed, and powerful in nature.

Kali's strength was not just in her ability to destroy but in her unapologetic existence. She was not bound by the expectations of being likable or manageable. She did not fit into the neat categories of dutifulness or devotion that society often ascribes to femininity. Kali was, instead, a celebration of pure, unbridled power—a power that is both awe-inspiring and terrifying, beautiful in a way that defies the shallow standards of prettiness.

In the Tantric traditions that venerate her, Kali's fearsome appearance and association with blood and death are not seen as negatives but as symbols of her ability to confront the deepest fears and darkest aspects of existence. She is both spiritual and bodily, erotic and transcendent, embodying the complex dualities of life.

Kali's nature is ambivalent and multifaceted, much like the early depictions of female deities who were not confined to a single role or attribute. Unlike male gods who often represent specific, singular aspects of divinity, Kali, like other ancient goddesses, embodied the full spectrum of life—from creation to destruction, from nurturing to annihilation.

This duality makes Kali the feminist icon we need today. She is a reminder that true female strength is not about conforming to societal norms but about embracing all aspects of one's identity. Kali's story is a powerful counter-narrative to the demure, submissive ideals of womanhood that have been propagated for centuries. Her ferocity, which even Shiva, the great destroyer, could not match, was long kept hidden or downplayed because it challenged the patriarchal status quo.

However, Kali's actions are not about dominating Shiva or anyone else. They are about expressing the uncontainable force of nature itself—a force that dances in victory, that celebrates its own existence without needing to apologize or justify itself. Kali's strength is not performative; it is inherent, an expression of the wild, untamed aspects of the universe that exist beyond human comprehension or control.

Choosing Kali as an icon is not about reclaiming the right to be aggressive or fierce. It is about embracing the full spectrum of what it means to be powerful, to be a woman, to exist without the need for approval or validation from the world. Like Kali, it is about simply being—unapologetically, fiercely, and completely.

## Hidimba

The story of Hidimba Devi, traditionally told as a tale of love and loyalty, can be reimagined as a narrative of a woman's strength, independence, and defiance of societal norms.

In the Kamyaka forest, where darkness and danger loomed, Hidimba was more than just a demoness or a sister following her brother's commands. She was a woman of fierce will and unyielding spirit, capable of making her own choices even when bound by familial duty. When Hidimba first laid eyes on Bhima, it wasn't merely infatuation that drove her to him, but the recognition of her own agency—her right to choose her destiny.

Hidimba's decision to propose marriage to Bhima wasn't an act of submission; it was a bold declaration of her desires in a world where women, especially those labeled as 'demonesses,' were expected to be subservient or treacherous. She defied her brother's orders, not out of weakness, but because she chose to follow her heart and forge a path that was her own. In revealing her true identity and warning Bhima of the danger, she asserted her autonomy, rejecting the role of a mere pawn in a patriarchal game of power.

Her agreement to Bhima's condition, that he would leave after their child was born, can be seen as an acceptance of her reality but not a resignation to it. Hidimba knew the strength she carried within, the power to survive and thrive even when left alone. The birth of her son, Ghatotkacha, marked not just the fulfillment of a marital contract, but the continuation of her legacy—a legacy of resilience, maternal power, and unwavering courage.

When Bhima left, Hidimba did not wallow in abandonment. Instead, she channeled her energy into raising her son, teaching him the ways of the warrior, and instilling in him the values of strength and honor. She didn't wait for a man to rescue or support her; she embodied the role of both mother and protector, ensuring that her son grew up strong and noble.

Hidimba's story, from this perspective, becomes a powerful feminist narrative—one of a woman who defied the roles assigned to her, who made her own choices, and who, despite the constraints of her society, carved out a life of strength, independence, and dignity. In this reimagining, Hidimba is not just a sidelined character in the epic of the Pandavas; she is a heroine in her own right, embodying the essence of female power and resilience.

# CHAPTER 7
# LOST IN TIME

With the passage of time, the meaning of the Rig Vedic hymns changed. They saw a number of different interpretations and even misinterpretations. Because of all these changes, It's easy to assume that the limitations imposed on women were rooted in the ancient texts themselves. But a deeper dive reveals an entirely different reality—one where women held agency, autonomy, and respect in ways that might surprise the modern reader. From festivals that celebrated their freedom of choice, to laws that safeguarded their dignity, these stories reflect a past where women were active participants in shaping the cultural and social fabric of their communities.

Yes. There were so many examples that were lost in time. In this chapter, we will learn about some of them. We will see how women were actually treated and what all works they were involved in.

## Samana Festival

In the Rig Veda, we find the mention of many hymns and verses that give us an insight about the rituals and culture of the ancient period. It is an important source of our understanding of life, which existed centuries ago. Historians have been deciphering and understanding the original meaning of these verses, which lost their charm over the period of time. These were altered and misinterpreted by different scholars of the later times.

But we still consider the Rig Veda as a reliable source. The Rig Vedic text also provides us knowledge about women of that age, their nature, and their situation. When flipping through the leaves of the text, we get to witness many hymns mentioning women and practices that were carried out at that time. One such mention is of the Samana Festival.

Different scholars have come up with different interpretations of the festival, but the most common one explains it as a recreational festival. Smana was a social festival, and there was no religious angle attached to it. It was a celebration that was attended by all sorts of people. It was seen as an opportunity to meet old friends and new people. They used to see it as a meet and greet.

For young women, this festival was more than a mere meet and greet. It was seen as an opportunity to step out and meet strangers, especially men. They used to interact with different men. It was seen as a festival where they had the opportunity to find a partner for themselves. There was no restriction on them, and they were set free. It is also believed that women used to dress up well and used to decorate themselves in order to attend the festival. This mingling gave them a window to understand their requirements for a partner in a better way. They used to learn about themselves too. It was more than a social festival for them. It was a place to choose their future husband, their life partner.

Samana used to take place in winters. It is popularly believed that the festival used to happen at night. To accommodate all the people and the craftsmen, it used to happen in an open space. There were different corners that were allotted for the performing people, and in the center there used to be the ceremonial fire to keep the place warm. Samana used to begin when people gathered around the fire and lasted till next morning or until the ceremonial fire died out. Therefore, women used to get enough time to know different men and their likes and dislikes. This time between the gathering and until the fire lasted was the time when women were free to choose the right person for themselves.

## Women In The Mauryan Period

Throughout our history, women were considered inferior to men. They were seen as soft individuals, unfit for high-endurance activities that are better suited for men as per the societal norms.

The ancient past, which has been criticized for the downgrading of women's position, was actually the era where they were respected more, so much so that they were even considered fit for the posts of sepoys! It was actually the time when women were seen as individuals who were on par with men in every domain.

It took us a really long time to accept women as beings with the capability of doing anything and everything, where high endurance work was no expectation. We can understand it with the fact that it took 45 years for our country to allow women to be part of the Indian Army.

The Mauryan Empire, which was a pan-India empire and ruled from 322 BCE to 185 BCE, was the first to appoint women to the posts of sepoys and bodyguards. We find mention of women's roles and the vibrant picture of their rights from the literary accounts of Arthashastra by Kautilya and even some of the Greek travelers who visited the Empire, like Meghasthenese.

In Arthashastra, written by Kautilya, we find details of how women used to protect the king, and he was taken care of by a troop of women archers known as the Striganairdhenvibhih. These women used to assist the king, beginning in the morning when the king used to get out of bed. They used to act as bodyguards and had the duty of protecting him round the clock. In the empire, women were considered capable and were assigned such a high priority and risky task.

Indica by Megasthenes comes in support of the grounds provided by the Arthashastra. According to the writings of Megasthenese, women in ancient India were equipped with weapons. They knew how to use them and kept the weapons to themselves. He even throws light on the role of women as guards who accompanied the king while he went on hunt in his chariot. These women used to carry a bow and arrow with them.

Apart from women serving as bodyguards and sepoys, Arthashashtra also mentions women as ascetics in the empire. The text mentions two types of ascetics: Parivrajakas and Bhiksukis. The former were the women who were either Brahmin or were widows, while in the later type, these were the women who had either shaved their heads or belonged to Jainism or Buddhism sects. As per Kautilya, the writer of the Arthashashtra, these women were excellent spies. They were vigilant and were often employed to examine the state officials.

Women of every industry were respected in the empire. Talking about the industry, the spinning and weaving industries played an important role in the lives of the Mauryan women. These industries even find their mention in the Sutradhyaksa chapter of the Arthashashtra. The text also states the honor of women who worked in these industries were protected.

Arthshastra states that the honor and chastity of women working in the weaving sector were to be protected at all costs. The text states that anyone who used to even look at the faces of the working women was punished. They had to pay a fine for their unacceptable actions. The wages of the women workers were taken as an important factor. The women who used to work in the royal factories or regular factories were paid the wages without any delay.

This highlights the degree of importance that was given to the honor of women. Their economic interests, as well as their security, held immense positions during that time.

When seen through the lens of economy, women of the Mauryan empire were not limited to the boundaries of the spinning and weaving sector. Even though it was a major contributor in the lives of women, they were also engaged in agricultural activities.

During the Mauryan period, prostitution as an occupation finds its mention in the history of the empire. Women who were involved in the occupation were called Ganikas. These women were provided with certain sets of rights and were given protection by the state in return for their services too. When they were young and used to offer their services, the ransom price was fixed at 24,000 panas. But they were taken care of even after getting old. They were appointed as Matrakas or nurses to other Ganikas. They were allowed to work in the spinning and weaving industry as well. Surprisingly, there were rules and regulations related to the matter of inheritance for them too. In the Mauryan Empire, after the death of a Ganika, the first nominee used to be her daughter. In case of absence of a daughter, the property was passed to the mother of the Ganika. When both were absent, in that scenario the property was confiscated by the empire.

Prostitution, which is prevalent even in today's world, holds no comparison to what was in that time. The rights of the Ganikas and the services that were provided to them once they became old can be seen as an inspiration for today's regulatory bodies.

## Gandharva Vivah

Marriage as an institution has been seen as an important affair of human life. Post the independence of India in 1947, we saw the crafting of laws providing directions and specifically tackling the disputes emerging out of marriage. The Hindu Marriage Act of 1955 and the Divorce Act, which was amended in 2001, were steps taken in this direction. We even have the Special Marriage, which came in 1954 to protect the rights of interfaith couples.

All these post-independence laws highlight the importance of marriage. Not just in recent times; there were many rules that had guided the institution in the past as well. We find the mention of different types of marriage in ancient texts too. One such type was Gandharva Vivah.

So what was Gandharva Vivah?

Gandharva Vivah finds its mention in many ancient texts, including the Dharma Sutras and the Griha Sutras. It is one of the eight classical kinds of marriages that were prevalent at that time. This vivah was not based on parental consent but mutual feelings and was prevalent and widely accepted by the society at large. Mutual consent and freedom of choice were given utmost importance.

In the Dharma Sutra, Baudhayana comments, **"Gandharvamapyeke prashansanti sarvesham snehanugatvat,"** which means that Gandharva marriage is praised by everyone because it is based on mutual affection. Even in the Kamasutra by Vatsayana, Gandharva Vivah has been highlighted for its positive effects. Kamasutra mentions that because the vivah is based on previous love, there are greater chances of the couple living happily.

In ancient India, women were given free hand in choosing their life partners. On the occasions of fairs, festivals, etc., when the whole village used to come together and join, young women of the society were allowed to meet and greet with the men of the society. This meet and greet allowed all the young ladies to understand the nature and life of the person they found attractive or approachable. Their conversations with the males allowed them to know them as a person and whether they possessed the qualities they wanted in their partner. It was the discretion of the women to choose the perfect 'husband' for themselves.

The union was solely based on the love and compassion that the couple had towards each other.

Apart from the mutual consent, there were certain simple rules that were followed for a successful Gandharva vivah. These rules included:

- The exchange of garlands between the couple should be made with fresh rose flowers only.
- The exchange of garlands should happen under a tree.
- The marriage ceremony used to happen only in the daytime and never during the night.
- The presence of a priest wasn't necessary, but certain vows were taken by the couple.

We find many examples of texts and plays that depict the Gandharva Vivah being carried out. One such example is the famous play of **Abhigyana Shakuntalam** by Kalidasa. Here Shakuntala undergoes Gandharva union with Dushyashan.

Another mention can be found in Brihatkatha, which is a huge collection of stories within stories. In most of the stories here, the princess had the option to choose and live with her life partner. The male here generally belonged to the lower status. Dashakumaracarita, a novel by Dandin, is one such example here.

Ancient texts also find the mention of divorce. One such mention is found in the Arthashastra, written by Kautilya. Arthashastra, which was written in the time of the Mauryan Empire, mentions **paraspara dveshat-moksha,** which means 'for freedom from mutual enmity'. It upholds the right of women to leave their husbands if they are found to be of bad character. Apart from this, they are allowed to leave their husband, who remains absent for a really long time, without any explanation. Men, on the other hand, were even punished if they remarried another woman for no reason. Though they were allowed to remarry if they had no children from their wives. Women were not barred from remarrying. If the husband of any woman remained absent without any reason or explanation, they were allowed to look for another partner. Even widows were allowed to remarry!

Kamasutra also supported widow remarriage. It said that any widow is free to choose their new life partner. Even the Rig Veda supports widow remarriage in its famous 'Burial Hymn.'

From all the information that is available to us in the context of Gandharv Vivah, we can conclude that women of ancient India had the right to choose their life partners. It was their decision, and no male was allowed to interfere in it. Even family members were barred from intervening in the subject of marriage. The mutual liking was the guiding force, and this allowed women to choose the best life partner and to spend their lives with them.

## Vedas On Sati

With the passage of time after the Vedic society, things changed for women, certain discriminations, limitations emerged. The sad part was that the blame was given to the ancient texts for the plight of the women, their reinterpretations happened in a way that led to ostracization of women at different levels. The lack of complete knowledge tarnished the essence of the Vedic hymns.

Over the period of time, after the Vedas were written, different scholars came and made different interpretations about the hymns. The meanings were changed as per their understanding, which was shaped highly by their will. Between all this reinterpretation and misinterpretation, many of the Vedic hymns lost their original meaning.

With time, the evil practices grew behind the veil of the Vedas. One such practice was Sati, where widows were burned alive within the funeral fire of her husband. People were so blinded by the concept of male dominance that no one even bothered to see the practice through the lens of humanity.

But was it actually the fault of Vedas? Do we really find the mention of an inhumane practice such as sati in the holy texts?

The answer here is NO.

The Vedas were never in support of Sati; instead, they mentioned the opposite of that. They asked the woman, who had lost her husband, to move forward in life with new light and possibilities. Sati meant something totally different from what it was understood to be.

Let's look at an example :

**इयंनारी पतिलोकं वृणाना तनपद्य उप त्वा मर्त्यप्रेमि्। तवश्वंपुराणमनुपालयन्ती स्यिैप्रजांद्रतवणंचेह धेतह॥**

**iyaṃ nārī patilokaṃ vṛṇānā nipadya upa tvā martya pretam. viśvaṃ purāṇamanupālayantī tasyai prajāṃ draviṇaṃ ceha dhehi.**

The core of this shloka deals with the liberation of the devoted wife and her getting permission to stay in this world of living beings. Not just that the shloka asks the world of living beings to permit her to attain wealth and progeny.

We can understand and conclude from his shloka that the Vedas have been asking the world to allow the women to live in this world even after the passing away of her husband. The tone of this mantra also makes it clear that it is the responsibility of the people of this world to make the lady respectfully turn away from her dead husband.

Oh! Departed one! This lady being desirous of attaining the world of the (you) husband is intensely staying in your proximity (near the dead body). And she follows (this) dharma of a (married) woman that is continuing since time immemorial (desiring proximity of the husband always). To such a devoted wife grant permission to stay in this world of living beings and also permit her to attain (your)(pre-existing) progeny and wealth.

Another Mantra from the Vedas -

**उदीर्ष्यनाययति जीवलोकतमासुमिमुपशेष एतह। हस्तग्रिास्य तदतधषोस्त्वमित् पर्त्ुजयतनत्वमतिसम्बि्व॥**

**udīrṣva nāryabhi jīvalokamitāsumetamupaśeṣa ehi. hastagrābhasya**

**didhiṣostvametatpatyurjanitvamabhisambabhūva.**

Hey Lady! You are lying near the body of the husband from where life has departed. Get up from there and come towards the world of living beings. Attain the status of wife of a man whose desires to hold your hand and marry (you) again.

In essence, the above manta deals with the concept of widow remarriage, which in later times was seen as a sin. The mantra also highlights that there is life and happiness for the wife of the deceased husband in this world.

By keeping the above two mantras in mind, we can understand the gravity of manipulation that happens with the essence and the real meaning of the same. The original value faded away with time and ended up being an unimaginably painful sin committed by society against women.

In today's world, thankfully Sati has been deemed illegal. From the above mentioned instance, we can understand the roots of other evils. The society that has been progressing on different grounds must also take into account the actual facts and statements and should reflect upon them. We, as a part of this society, should play an active role in seeking the actualities and the truth.

## Streedhan- The Right Of Every Women

The term 'Streedhan' is made up of two words: 'stree', which means a woman, and 'dhan', which means property. This was the concept that allowed women of ancient times to hold authority over their belongings. It included all types of assets, from moveable to immovable, currency, ornaments, etc.

The first mention of 'stridhan' is found in Manusmriti. It included all the gifts that were given to the woman before or after her marriage or even at the time of childbirth by her father, mother, brother, husband, father-in-law, or any family member. But the modern evils abstained the women of society to acquire their paternal property.

For a married woman, streedhan was divided into two types, namely Saudayika and non-Saudayika gifts. There is a major difference between these two. In the Saudayika gift, all the assets that the woman attained before her marriage or after the widowhood belonged completely to her, and these were the gifts that she attained by self-effort or mechanical skills. Due to this reason, women had complete freedom over all the assets, and they possessed complete authority in terms of their disposal.

The non-Saudayika gifts were the assets that the woman used to get at the time or after their marriage. In this case, they shared the rights with their husband. They were not the sole authority taking the decisions. For the disposal, they had to seek permission from their partner too.

The Saudayika gifts provided women with complete authority, and the non-Saudayika gifts offered them partial authority. But women had the say in both.

Sridhan, which was offered to the women, was seen as a sign of respect in the ancient society. All the gifts they received from their parents and the in-laws were under their authority. All the gifts give us the reflection of women in the new home.

The concept that emerged with a positive motive behind it was later turned into an obligation and manifested itself in the form of Dowry. A sage of ancient India named, Baudhyana, even went to extremes to state that, the husband should pay a dowry to the bride's family, rather than it being the opposite.

The in-laws started seeing the newlywed bride as a source of wealth. This put pressure on the bride and her family to arrange all the demands of the in-laws. The atrocities against women increased, and we have seen cases of women being burned and even tortured in every possible way. To tackle this deteriorating situation of women, the government intervened in 1961 when it legislated the Dowry Prohibition Act, but despite the efforts, the cases continued to be in the limelight.

There are many other examples present in history that have proven to be in favor of women's empowerment and support, like women participating in local markets and trade, managing household economies; in some sects of Hinduism, women took part in public rituals and festivals where they mingled with men; women in royal courts had opportunities to interact with male courtiers, advisors, and diplomats. Queens and princesses often played influential roles in politics and diplomacy, which involved significant mingling with men.

Even after all this evidence which is present in the ancient texts, the texts on which society has been relying upon, for most of the people, women are merely a puppet who dances on the direction of the males. You must think, if this was the case, then where did we go wrong? Why did the women face all the discrimination? Well, things went south when the hold of these texts came in the hands of later priests. The misinterpretation made the actual essence submerge in the ocean of patriarchy.

Now that we know the problem, where is the solution? If you ask me, it lies in your thinking and your willingness to find the roots of the evils. When you dig deeper, you'll find a society that has catered to its women in the best possible way. When you'll see the history after removing the dust of male dominance, you'll explore the truths that were never told.

## Ritu Kala Sanskara

In ancient India, women used to celebrate an intricate part of their life, which was a sign of adulthood and was an important aspect for the continuation of human species in this world - Menstruation. The word which was burdened with many taboos and restrictions in the later times was actually a celebrated affair. It was seen as a sign of a girl attaining maturity and becoming a woman. Girls who got their periods for the first time were celebrated and given special treatment in the form of Ritu Kala Sanskara.

This Sanskara has been believed to start between 1500 BCE and 1200 BCE and we can find it happening in many parts of South India even today. It began as a ceremony which was attended by all the family members to celebrate the new chapter of a girl's life, her womanhood.

Ritu Kala Samskara played an important role in women's life. In ancient India it was more than the celebration of physical changes that follows menstruation but also the emotional surge that happens. It was a ritual that was and has been comforting women about their menstrual cycles, to remind them that they are special and about their power to be the force that maintains the human race.

During the Ritu Kala Samaskara, all the family members used to gather to bless the girl child who had entered the phase of womanhood in her life. There were many rituals included in the celebration along with the draping of Saree. Saree, which is seen as a garment mostly associated with women, is used here to make the girl feel the essence of growing up, the emotion of entering into womanhood. There are many other rituals associated with the Sanskara that are believed to purify the girl's body and soul and prevent them from evil forces.

The girl is given a ritual bath in the first place to begin her new journey. This is followed by her wearing new clothes, which are a new saree and choli, and even in some cases, jewelry. The ritual bath is believed to purify the physical body and the spiritual mind of the girl. This is the first time that the girl wears a saree and it marks a new phase of her life.

Ritual bath is followed by friends and relatives applying turmeric and kumkum on the forehead and other body parts of her body. Turmeric is used because of its antiseptic properties and kumkum is believed to bring good luck in her life. After this, the newly transformed woman moves forward to seek the blessings of her elders and other members. This is where she is guided by the relatives about her upcoming future and responsibilities as well as the changes that she would now face in life.

After seeking the blessings of her elders, it's time for the girl to seek blessings of the almighty. She carries out puja followed by offerings to the god. The puja is performed as it is considered auspicious and is believed to bring good fortune to the girl. Well, this is very different from the beliefs that emerged in the later times. Even in today's India, many women are still not allowed to enter temples or perform puja when on their periods. The sanskara was finally wrapped up with a community meal.

This was the beauty of Hindu culture, where women were appreciated and womanhood was celebrated. Over the period of time, this ritual lost its charm and periods emerged as a topic not to be discussed in public. With time, womanhood became stressful for all the women because of the evils that flooded the society.

Ritu Kala Samskara was enthusiastically celebrated especially by women. They used to take pride in entering the new journey, warmly welcoming the new phase of their lives. It was seen as an empowering ritual which made women more comfortable and open in the society. It was when they used to publicly announce their first periods.

The ritual involved all the family members, who used to celebrate their daughter, her first periods. They used to appreciate her journey as a young kid and would openly guide her about her upcoming life.

It was the time when there was no taboo associated with menstruation and women together used to celebrate womanhood. It was a free culture where the girl was reminded of her power and her capabilities. It was the ritual which made the girl who just entered a new phase understand that she is important and that she matters.

# CHAPTER 8

## Amazing Women Of Medieval India

At the dawn of Medieval India, thoughts, cultural practices, societal roles, and perceptions of women were all shifting. By the end of the ancient period, significant evolution had already taken place, setting the stage for a new era filled with startling changes across multiple domains. Amid this evolution, however, certain social evils began to take shape. Misinterpretations of sacred texts emerged, twisting original teachings to justify restrictive practices and rigid hierarchies. Invasions introduced new challenges, further intensifying the societal pressures women faced.

The Mughal period, too, brought its own set of complexities. While society was marked by grandeur and prosperity, many deep-seated issues persisted, limiting women's roles and agency. Yet, amid these constraints, many women stood apart, refusing to succumb to societal expectations and instead working to change the tide. In the face of such adversities, they embodied resilience, courage, and determination, setting examples that resonate even today. Their stories inspired people of their time and remain a powerful source of motivation for women in the contemporary world. In this section, we will explore the lives of these remarkable women, drawing inspiration from their strength as they navigated and rose above the trials of their time.

## Nur Jahan

Nur Jahan, originally named Mihrunnisa, who later became an exceptional queen in Mughal history, has many stories associated with her, explaining her rise in power. One such story tells that Nur Jahan's parents were robbed after her birth. They lost all their wealth to it and were left with no option but to leave Nur Jahan by the side of the road as they couldn't afford a third child. Grief followed them as they moved away from her. They felt horrible for taking such an inhumane step and went back to pick her up, not certain whether they would see her again. But to their surprise, they found Nur Jahan sitting exactly where they left her, safe next to a black snake. Anecdotes like these have been used even for her later life to display her natural charm.

ig.1 1620 by Abu'l Hasan (Harvard Art Museu

Source- Journal by Maggie Schuster

Mihrunnisa was born to her Persian parents in Kandahar. She came to India with her parents, who were trying to run away from poverty under the rule of Shah Ismail II (r. 1576–1577) in Iran. They were trying to seek asylum in India, which was being ruled by Akbar. They had hopes because many of their relatives had already done it in the past.

The meeting of Nur Jahan and Jahangir is believed to have happened in 1611 during Navroz, or the Persian New Year. Nur Jahan's first marriage was with a Persian adventurer named Sher Afghan in 1594, with whom she had a daughter, her only child, as she didn't have any children with Jahangir.

Jahangir married Nur Jahan in 1611 after meeting her during Navroz. To commemorate the new bond, Jahangir added a huge stone basin in his Agra fort, likely for wine, similar to the one he commissioned in Kabul. Jahangir's memoirs, although they didn't mention his marriage with Nur Jahan, mention her 17 times. For instance, he wrote about his short-lived promise to give up on hunting.

Jahangir had his full support for Nur Jahan, and this is evident by the fact that he made her the financial advisor after the death of her father. He also allowed her to mint coins in her name, an honor that was reserved for the emperors only. Few coins that survived from her reign were made up of gold and silver. They bear the names of the king and the queen on opposite sides in Persian script. They serve as living evidence of the unique reign of Nur Jahan, the only Mughal queen who had the privilege to mint coins in her name.

The title 'Nur Jahan' meaning 'Light of the World', which was given by Jahangir to his beloved queen, also depicts his inclination towards her. Before the title of Nur Jahan, she was given the title of 'Nur Mahal' which means the 'Light of the Palace', which the queen held until 1616. She and Jahangir ruled together until his death in 1627.

During her reign, she, along with the mother of Jahangir, were the key players involved in commissioning the architecture. This was notable because Jahangir was himself not at all involved and interested in the affairs of the empire. To fill the void, the royal women played a pivotal role in construction commissioning during his reign.

One such project was Nurmahal caravanserai, which was commissioned by Nur Mahal in 1618 and took two years to complete. Nurmahal was built in Punjab. Believes are that the location was dear to Nur Jahn because of the memories of her childhood attached to that place, but if seen from an economic lens, speaks a completely different story. The beautiful monument was built on a strategic road joining Agra and Kashmir, which was an important trade route. The positioning of the caravanserai along the route assured the court of Jahangir a constant flow of tariffs and taxes, which were collected from the travelers. The income so generated provided Nur Jahan a free hand in commissioning more architecture, leaving a mark of her legacy behind.

Interestingly, Mundy in his book attributed the construction of caravanserai to Nur Jahn, but many later writings attribute it to Jahangir. This difference is the result of perceptions and perspectives that different cultures had towards the subject of authority. But there is a living witness that speaks the true story—the inscriptions on the Nurmahal. They confirm that it was the economic and political mind of Nur Jahan.

**Image- Inscriptions on Nur Jahan's Nurmahal**

Source- punjabjalandhar.info

Nur Jahan diverted all the wealth that was derived from trades, gifts, and even from her family fortune in the construction of architecture. Yet, her political influence at the time of her death was nil. What made such a shrewd woman end up in such a plight? Well, it was her stepson, Shah Jahan. The increasing power of Nur Jahan came as contention between her and Shah Jahan. The problem escalated to the extent that Nur Jahan was sent to exile by Shah Jahan until she died 18 years later. The contention was because Nur Jahn wanted Shahriyar, Jahangir's son, who was married to her daughter, to come to the throne after his father's death. This idea was not liked by Shah Jahan. This resulted in Shah Jahan's revolt, which took place shortly after the death of Nur Jahan's father. These two events began to destabilize the empire.

Nur Jahan was removed from court, and even the legacy that she built was under threat. Most of the coins that the Mugal queen minted in her name, a rare heritage of her reign, were destroyed by Shah Jahan. This was the end of her story, and life came a complete circle to her.

## Begum Samru: Warrior, Diplomat, And Queen

In the 18th century, when feuds were arising in the Mughal empire, the war of succession was taking over all the glory, and the turbulence was shaking the roots of the Mughals, there emerged a woman who was filled with courage and smartness named Begum Samru.

## Early Life As A Courtesan And Later A Captain

She was born as Farzana Zebunnisa and became an orphan at a very young age. Her life was filled with hardships; Samru was forced to live with a courtesan in Delhi. As a result, she learned the art of entertainment, primarily for her survival, very early. When she was a teenager, she met Walter Joseph Reinhardt, a Franco-German mercenary. He was in his forties when he met Begum Samru, and despite their age difference, she initially became his companion and later his wife.

Image- Portrait of Begum Samru
Source- Storytrails

Her life took a sharp turn in 1778 when her husband, Joseph Reinhardt, passed away. Many believed her life to end the moment her husband left the world, but little did they know that it was the beginning of the life of a warrior, a queen. Samru stood up for herself, defying all the odds and expectations of society; she assumed the command of her husband's army.

No one at that time would have thought of her as a commanding officer. A woman who was barely 5 feet was definitely in stark contrast from the conventional-looking warriors. But she proved herself. In the world that watched the steadily declining Mughal empire, Samru held her chin up and emerged as a brave warrior and a diplomatic leader.

She knew her steps and the direction she was moving in. As a fierce and courageous warrior, she used to lead the battle herself as the head of the cavalry, and this act of hers made her earn the loyalty of all those in her troop.

## A Diplomat Who Saved Delhi

She was not only a courageous warrior but a pragmatic woman. This combination graced her diplomatic tactics, which helped her in negotiating with many leaders. With her skills, she even reached a settlement with Sikh General Baghel Singh in 1783, at the time when he was ready to attack Delhi. This smart move of the diplomatic woman cemented her position as a capable leader

Saving Delhi, for her empire, was just a trailer of her skills. Samru in later years displayed her boldness and diplomatic mindset at various events. In 1787, when Red Fort was surrounded by the army of Rohilla chieftain Ghulam Abd al Qadir Ahmed Khan, the fierce begum launched an attack that rooted the army of the opposition and successfully rescued the Mughal Emperor Shah Alam II. Impressed by Samru, Shah Alam II gave her the title of "Farzand-e-Azizi," which translates to Beloved Daughter.

## Woman With Smart Moves

Despite her growing charisma and power, she always kept her eye on ground realities. In the time when the power began to shift to the Britisher's side, many of the rulers were losing their kingdoms. In such a situation, she made a smart decision and swiftly aligned with the European powers. In a time when kingdoms were falling in the hands of Britishers, she secured the autonomy of her kingdom and her throne, displaying her political awareness and decisions.

Begum Samru etched her name in the leaves of history when she became the first and only native Catholic ruler of

Statue of Begum Samru, Basilica of Our Lady of Graces, Sardhana, UP

Source- Storytrails

her time. It was in 1781 that she converted to Christianity and adopted the name Joanna Nobilis Sombre. After her conversion, she commissioned the construction of the Basilica of Our Lady of Graces, which still stands to date and is a perfect example of a fusion of European and Mughal styles of architecture. Whether her move to convert to Christianity was a personal choice or part of her strategic move is not known, but her decision made her gain a unique place in history.

## Legacy Of Warrior Samru..

The life of Begum Samru was filled with a strong spirit of warrior and intelligence. Her actions and decisions made her rise to the level of a powerful leader who had displayed her skills in every domain of kingship. Her extraordinary achievements made her story an inspiration for many women. Her dedication and determination, along with her smart mind and swift calculations, left a strong imprint on history.

The fierce queen took her last breath in 1836 when she was 83 and left the legacy, which continues to be a testimony of her bravery and indomitable spirit.

## Gulbadan Begum

It is the story from the time when Babur had laid the foundation of the Mughal Empire after the third war of Panipat. The world at that time was turbulent as powers were shifting their balance. In that unstable world, Gulbadan Begum was born in the year 1523. Born in the royal Mughal family, the daughter of Babur was born to witness the rise and fall of the most powerful empire of that time. Even though the history textbooks have provided us with a good idea of the Mughal Empire, we know a little about the princess, who was an adventurous spirit and a writer too. It was she who paved the way for herself amid the tense times; it was she who wrote books for the emperors; it was her that we have historical records that describe a lot about that era–it was Gulbadan Begum.

## The World She Was Born In

While growing up, Gulbadan had seen political decisions and battles, followed by the stories that narrated how bravely her father fought and won over the enemies. Being a Mugahl princess, she was always surrounded by the environment of war and attacks, and all these left an imprint on the little princess.

Growing up, she came across the rules and regulations of Harem, a place that was dedicated to women.

Brought by the Turkish dynasties for the first time, Harems were of different kinds. In the context of Mughal India, harems encompassed different categories of female inhabitants based on their status and roles:

First was the Legal Wives ("Begums") who were the officially wedded wives married under Islamic law, often with high dowries. They held a respected position in the harem and were prioritized over other women. They had greater rights and could demand more attention from the ruler. Second were the free Inferior Wives ("Aghas") who were married to the ruler but without the same legal or social standing as the "Begums." While not always from aristocratic backgrounds, these wives enjoyed some privileges, but were regarded as lesser than the primary wives. Lastly, Concubines ("Aghachas," "Paristaran," "Khawas-i-Khidmatgaran")who were women slaves or captives kept primarily for the ruler's pleasure without legal marriage. Their status depended on factors such as lineage, and they were often evaluated based on physical appearance and refinement. However, if a concubine bore the ruler a child, she could gain some rights and privileges, although she was not entirely free.

| Status | Rank | Freedom | Salary |
|---|---|---|---|
| Legal wives as per Islamic law | Begum | Free | Rs. 40-50/ month |
| Favorite women of King but not wives | Aghas | Free | Rs. 40-10/ month |
| Concubine | Aghacha | Slave | NA |

Here we are talking about the 1st kind of Harem. There is a common belief by many scholars that the first category of women in the Harems used to assert their influence in administrative tasks. Examples of such women are Gulbadam Begum herself, Maham Anga, who was the foster mother of emperor Akbar. She was a political advisor to Akbar and eventually became the de-facto ruler who actively influenced court politics and administration. This side of the Harem states that recommendations from the women of Harem carried considerable weight. To enhance their prestige, women were given high titles by the king such as 'Miriyam Makhani' meaning the mary of both the worlds. This title was given to the mother of Akbar. We find many other titles like 'Mumtaz Mahal', 'Shah Begum', etc that signifies their position in the life of the king and thereby their influence in the royal scenario.

There is a common belief by many researchers and scholars that harem provided women the space to get involved in political matters of the empire. For example, Rekha Misra in her book - Women in Mughal India talks about the Chingizi-Timurid traditions and how it gave females the opportunity to exercise their power. Women even had some gained control over the financial resources and were involved in different economic activities by using Eunuchs as their agents.

It was here that Gulbadan Begum began to understand the intricate web of relationships and how the space between happiness and sorrow was filled by the women of the harem. Spending her formative years there, she was used to the confined movement between the tents and the citadel, but Gulbadan's spirit was independent. It was a confined world inside the harem, with women and their hierarchy, where they would discuss things together, would console each other, and would stick together. It was in this world that Gulbadan Begum found her own way to assert her independence.

## The Unseen Life Of Gulbadan Begum

We have so much evidence of marriages in the Mughal World; it was a well-celebrated affair. But Gulbadan Begum was of different views. She was the one who wanted to keep her life concealed. We do not find any mention of her marriage but from a brief remark made by her brother Humayun in 1539, when he came back from the Battle of Chausa.

When he returned to Agra, he noticed Gulbadan wearing a muslin lachaq, which was a cap for the royal brides. It is from here that we know that Gulbadan was married to her cousin Khizr Khwaja Khan. This was the level of secrecy and privacy that Gulbadan Begum maintained. A woman who has not been known and lived in a rather secretive world, but lived a life filled with adventure and courage.

The queen, who loved to keep her affairs private, was a writer too. It was she who wrote about the lives of the first three Mughal emperors, a task that may have not been performed by any other women of that time. She wrote it on the request of her nephew, Akbar, and mentioned the wars and campaigns and explained how the world used to look at such times through her lens. Not just that, she even described the personal aspects of the royal family—the celebrations, relationships, and tensions. In her writings we even find mention of the gift-giving ceremonies, the one that even followed after the victory of Babur over Ibrahim Lodhi. From here, we can infer the situations that existed in the domestic sphere.

From the literacy record belonging to Gulbadan Begum, historians have been able to understand the extent of family involvement and the interpersonal relationships that prevailed in the Mughal Empire.

## The Pilgrimage To Mecca

Gulbadan Begum is also known for her pilgrimage to Mecca, which was more than a spiritual journey for her.

It was in the year 1577, Gulbadan Begum along with Salima Sultan Begum and many other royal women, began their pilgrimage from Surat. They sailed through the Arabian

Sea, where the waters welcomed them with countless challenges. Her journey was not at all easy, but Gulbadan Begum gave it all and completed her pilgrimage.

## Breaking The Cage - Always A Free Spirit

After the pilgrimage with other royal women, when she stepped on her homeland, she sensed a difference. The empire was now under the firm control of Akbar. There was also a more established Harem structure in place, which was made up of red sandstone. It was a confined structure, which wasn't comfortable for the women who had been moving between the citadel and the tents for a really long time. The new Harem structure was praised by many, including Abul Fazl, who was Akbar's chronicler, but Gulbadan couldn't see the Harem in the same way.

Harem was no longer seen as a free place by her; it had become a restrictive structure, but still it couldn't cage Gulbadan's freedom. She kept writing, which was the reflection of her life experiences and which even now stands as a testament to her free spirit.

## The Legacy Of Gulbadan Begum

The little girl who was born in a time that saw a change in power dynamics, grew up to live her life the way she wanted. In a time where women were suppressed under the shadow of male power, Gulbadan Begum created opportunities for her expressions and fed her adventurous spirit with new experiences. Her story is not just of a Mughal princess but of a woman who lived a life that was inspiring and remarkable.

## Naiki Devi

Born to the king Kadamba of Goa, Naiki Devi evolved as the embodiment of courage when she defeated Muhammad Ghori. This is the story of the un-acclaimed warrior lady, a queen who stood up to protect her kingdom and used the amalgamation of her intelligence and strength to defeat the undefeated ruler.

Image- Naiki Devi
Source- The Better India

Naikia Devi was well trained in diplomacy, sword fighting, and many other subjects that are important for running a state. When she grew up, she got married to the Chalukyan prince Ajaypal. When she was married, she had no idea what history was holding for her.

After her marriage, she became the queen of Gujarat. She even gave birth to a baby boy, Mularaj II. The queen was living her regular life when, in 1175, she lost her husband. This came as a shock to the Chalukyan queen, who had an infant with her.

According to the norms of that time, the kingdom was to be handled and ruled by Mularaja II. But because he was a child at that time, Naiki Devi assumed the charge of the throne as Raj Mata. Her right over the throne was until Mularaja II was grown up. She took the responsibility as a regent with determination.

She was ruling the kingdom in the best possible way. Naiki Devi had been taught the craft of state diplomacy and functioning in her childhood. She was using her knowledge for the prosperity of her kingdom. Little did she know that a storm was waiting for her. Busy with managing the empire, she got to know that Muhammad Ghori was eyeing her kingdom.

Muhammad Ghori was an extremely fierce ruler who had an army filled with trained and skilled warriors driven by religious conviction. His eye was now on Anhilwara, the capital of the Chalukyan empire.

When Naiki Devi got to know about Ghori's intention, she knew she had to save her kingdom. In order to secure her empire, she opened diplomatic dialogues with the neighboring kingdoms. She requested assistance from the kings of nearby provinces. Many of them denied any ally, while others came up in support of Naiki Devi. She received aid from the leaders of the Naddula Chahamana clan, the Jalor Chahamana clan, and the Arbuda Paramara clan. They were all feudatories of the Chalukyas.

It is also believed that Muhammad Ghori sent the queen an opportunity to surrender. But the fierce queen didn't let the Islamic king deteriorate her confidence and bravery. She decided to fight.

After forming an alliance, Naiki Devi came up with a well-planned strategy. She gave thought to the conditions and decided to choose Gadaraghatta as her site of battle. Gadaraghatta, in present-day Sirohi District, was a rugged terrain.

When the army of Muhammad Ghroi came, the geography of the battlefield that Naiki Devi chose was unfamiliar to the troops. This gave the queen an edge over the odds. The battle was finally fought between the Rajput forces led by Naiki Devi and the army of Muhammad Ghori.

The fierce queen rode the battleground with her son tied to her lap. She fought until the troops of Muhammad Ghori were pushed back. The Chalukyan army emerged as the victorious force and defeated the army of Muhammad Ghori, an army that had made even the sultan of Multan kneel down. This battle became known as the Battle of Kasahrada.

It was a major defeat for Ghori. He attacked the kingdom, underestimating its power because it was being ruled by a woman. His defeat made him leave the battleground with few of his bodyguards. Not only that, he never looked again at the Chalukyan kingdom ever.

## Rani Durgawati

On October 5, 1524, on the auspicious day of Durgashtami, a daughter was born to Raja Salbahan of Ratha and Mahoba, a descendent of the Chandela dynasty. The child was named Durga, after the goddess of power and courage. At that time, the king had no idea that not just the name, but his daughter was born to rise to power too. Born in the fort of Kalinjar, located in today's

UP, Durgavati was born and was destined for greatness. Having her roots from the Chandelas, who were known for their courage. Little did this world at that time know that it was not the birth of a baby girl, but it saw the birth of a future warrior.

Image- Rani Durgavati

As she grew up, the marital alliances had been changed—from merely being relations runned by emotions, they were then for forming strategic alliances. When Durgavati turned 18, she was married to the king of the Gond kingdom of Garha-Katanga, King Sangram Shah. It was definitely more than a marriage; it was a pact that ensured the cementing of the trust and partnership of the two royal families. Chandelas and Gonds had shared a mutual respect for a long time, but this marital alliance allowed them to take a step further in their relationship.

The alliance strengthened the strength of the two kingdoms. But the alliance saw a tragic event in their timeline when Dalpat Singh died. He died early and left Durgavati to rule Garha-Katanga, which was known for its forests, forts, and army. Durgavati was a regent for their son, Bir Narayan, who was an infant at that time. The responsibility of protecting the boundaries of the vast kingdom was left on the shoulders of Queen Durgavati. With her infant by her side, Durgavati emerged as a capable leader who managed the sovereignty of her kingdom with utmost respect. With the passage of time, she even gained the confidence and loyalty of the court nobles when she successfully expanded the borders of her kingdom. It was under her rule that the kingdom flourished, and she proved herself as a potential ruler in every sense.

The kingdom of Garha-Katnga was under Ranidurgavti as her son was growing up. She was very dedicatedly governing the empire as a regent of her son, but with the growing Mughal expansion happening around, Garha-Katnga came under the target of Akbar. The emperor of the Mughals was ambitious and already had his eyes set on the kingdom of Durgavati. It was the time when she had the pressure of protecting her empire. The Mughals had already defeated the kingdoms of Rewa and Pnna, and this situation came as a real test for Rani Durgavati.

Kara-Manikpur, who was the Mughal Governor, initially proposed the establishment of friendly relations and trade establishments with the kingdom of Garha-Katnga. But his malicious intent behind the proposal couldn't stay hidden for a long time. His proposal was a tactic to gather information about the kingdom's potential—its treasure and cavalry. On gathering all the knowledge he wanted, Kara-Manikpur launched an attack on the kingdom in the year 1564. At this point, Rani Durgavati had no plans in hand; she was caught off guard and was even advised by her ministers to surrender. But Rani Durgavati stood up to her values;

she was ready to die with honor rather than spending life in shame. She didn't hesitate to launch a retaliatory attack on the Mughal forces. Even though she had 500 men with her, she guided her troops and prepared for the battle.

In a situation that was filled with pressure and stress, Rani Durgavati took pragmatic decisions and chalked down her strategy in the finest manner. Her knowledge of the geography of her kingdom allowed her to utilize the natural barriers that were available to her. Instead of a small force, she was ready with a strategic plan.

Fer's first move was to position her troops in Narhi. The reason she chose it was because it was covered by high hills and was flaked by Narmada and Gur. She placed her troops and waited for the attack by the army of Asaf Khan, which had a vast army loaded with infantry and cavalry. The moment the Mughal army entered, Rani Durgavati signaled for the execution of her plan. The moment her army received the permission of their queen, they attacked the Mughal forces from all sides. The battle saw severe casualties on the Mughal side, and as a result, the brilliant plotting by the queen made the Mughal forces retreat.

Rani Durgavati was alarmed by this sudden attack, and she wasn't ready to sit quite after that. After her victory over the Mughal intention in the first attack, she wanted to be prepared for securing her kingdom. As a result, Rani Durgavati proposed a night attack. She wanted to prevent the Mughals from basing into the narrow passage, a strategic point for the kingdom and its safety. But her proposal wasn't accepted by the generals, who were hesitant to rise against the Mughals. This hesitancy allowed the Mughal forces to come back strong the next day when Asaf Khan placed heavy guns into position.

The enemy was well-equipped, eyeing the fort and ready to attack any moment, but all this couldn't daunt the brave queen Durgavati. Even after knowing the consequences, she mounted on Sarman, her favorite elephant, and led her army. Gazing directly into the eyes of the enemy, she moved with courage and even successfully pushed back the Mughal forces thrice until Bir Naraym got severely injured. Her son was wounded, her army was fighting, and the Mughals were slowly holding their grip in the battle, but none of these could stop Rani Durgawati. She fought with all the courage that she had.

Rani Durgavati's bravery kept fueling the enthusiasm of her army until she was struck by two arrows, one of which pierced her neck. It was at this moment that she knew that the kingdom of Garha-Katanga had been lost. But she wasn't ready to face capture by the enemy and wanted to die with honor. She asked her elephant driver to kill her, but he had no courage to do so. As a result, Rani Durgavati wasn't left with any option but to kill herself. With two arrows already in her body, she used her blood-wrapped hands to take out her dragger. The woman of high values decided to die with honor, and using her dragger, she ended her life.

After the death of Rani Durgavati, the Mughals took control of the Garha-Katanga. It didn't happen swiftly. The capital of the empire, Chauragarh, was being protected by Bir Narayan, and it took a fierce battle between the Mughals and Bir Narayan for the falling of the guards of the capital.

Rani Durgavati has been praised by many future historians, her stories narrated with utmost respect. Abul Fazl mentioned her as a woman with beauty and courage. Her life story has been chronicled by the British too. British

Colonel Sleeman recognized her as one of the most revered sovereigns of Garha-Katanga.

To honor her, a memorial has been erected in Jabalpur. The memorial is the place where she fell when she killed herself. In 1983, the name of Jabalpur University was changed to Rani Durgavati University, and the year also saw the establishment of a museum in her name. In 1988, a postal stamp was issued to celebrate her bravery, and in 2018, the Indian Coast Guard named an Inshore Patrol Vessel 'ICGS Rani Durgavati' in her memory.

Rani Durgavati's sacrifice has been seen as a symbol of valor. Her story has been inspiring generations and has been reminding them of the price that has been paid by many in history to protect what we today own as a heritage. Even

A stamp issued in honour of Rani Durgavati in 1988. Image Source: Wikimedia Commons

Image- Postal stamp of Rani Durgavati
Source- Indian Culture, GoI

though the Mughals looted the kingdom after the death of the queen, they couldn't erase the mark of her bravery.

Due to constraints of time and space, we could not cover other women from this period. However, for a few of them we would like to make a special mention.

- **Maharani Jijabai:** Mother and guiding force behind Chhatrapati Shivaji Maharaj!
- **Rani Durgavati (1524–1564):** The queen of Gondwana (central India), she is remembered for her bravery in leading her army against the Mughal Emperor Akbar's forces. Though she ultimately lost her life in battle, her resilience and bravery are widely celebrated.
- **Rani Abbakka Chowta (1525–1570):** Queen of Ullal in Karnataka, she led a fierce resistance against the Portuguese, who sought to control the western coastal regions. Her strategies and knowledge of guerrilla warfare made it difficult for the Portuguese to establish dominance.
- **Rani Karnavati of Garhwal (17th Century):** Known as "Nakti Rani," she was the queen of Garhwal, now in Uttarakhand, and famously repelled a Mughal invasion led by Shah Jahan. She cleverly commanded her forces and defeated the much larger Mughal army.
- **Rani Ahilyabai Holkar (1725–1795):** Though she ruled slightly later, her legacy as the queen of the Malwa kingdom stands out. Ahilyabai was both a brilliant ruler and a skilled warrior, defending her kingdom from external threats and focusing on the welfare of her people.
- **Rani Chennabhairadevi (16th Century):** Known

as the "Queen of Pepper," she ruled over the coastal region of Karnataka and held off Portuguese forces for nearly 50 years. Her naval strategies were especially effective, and she ensured her kingdom thrived despite the European threat.

- **Rani Rudrama Devi (1262–1289):** One of the first female rulers of the Kakatiya dynasty in South India, she was known for her administrative skills and bravery in leading her army. She even adopted the male identity "Rudradeva Maharaja" to maintain her authority and inspire confidence in her people.
- **Rani Tarabai Bhonsle (1675–1761):** The Maratha queen played a crucial role in resisting Mughal forces after her husband, Chhatrapati Rajaram's death. Her leadership helped keep the Maratha Empire intact and safeguarded its legacy during a turbulent period
- **Rani Abbakka Chowta:** Queen of Ullal
- **Rani Karnavati:** Queen of Garhwal
- **Rani Chennabhairadevi:** Queen of the Tuluva Kingdom, Karnataka
- **Maharani Jindan Kaur:** Queen regent of the Sikh Empire
- **Maharani Lakshmibai of Jhansi:** Leader of the Indian Rebellion of 1857
- **Rani Velu Nachiyar:** Queen of Sivaganga, Tamil Nadu
- **Chand Bibi:** Queen regent of Ahmednagar and Bijapur Sultanate

- **Rani Kittur Chennamma:** Queen of Kittur in Karnataka
- **Rani Mangammal:** Queen regent of the Madurai Nayak Kingdom
- **Rani Avantibai:** Queen of Ramgarh, fought against British rule
- **Rani Udayamati:** Queen of the Solanki dynasty, known for building the Rani ki Vav stepwell
- **Rani Bhatiyani:** Revered warrior queen of Rajasthan
- **Rani Padmavati:** Queen of Chittor, known for her courage and sacrifice
- **Rani Bhopal Kaur:** Queen of the Jind princely state, fought against the British
- **Maharani Meenakshi:** Queen of the Nayak dynasty in Madurai
- **Bibi Dalair Kaur:** Sikh warrior who fought against Mughal forces
- **Maharani Sunity Devi:** Queen of Cooch Behar, an advocate for women's rights and education

# CHAPTER 9

# Concepts From Medieval India That Caught My Eye

During medieval India, the arrival of foreign dynasties like the Turks and Arabs brought with them distinct cultures, customs, and a fervent ambition to establish power. As these dynasties intermingled with the diverse heritage of the Indian subcontinent, they introduced new laws, rights, and traditions, creating a unique cultural mosaic. Though powerful and resilient, these early dynasties were ultimately overtaken by the Mughals, who built an empire grounded in administration, architecture, and ideology. However, despite the glory of the Mughal empire, there were systemic problems that affected the women of the society.

As these dynasties shifted power, some women from royal and noble households often wielded influence in ways that defied societal norms. They came up with concepts that reflected resilience, strategic alliances, and silent yet powerful agency—which are often overlooked in mainstream accounts of this period. In this chapter, we will explore these "Concepts from Medieval India," spotlighting the decisions of women who, despite the male-dominated society, carved out spaces of influence and autonomy. Through their actions, they turned the odds into opportunities, shaping the fabric of an era that sought to confine them, and left enduring legacies that continue to inspire.

## Makhfi - The 'Hidden' One..

Women in medieval India were known for their political and administrative hold in the kingdom, where they used to exert their ideas, thoughts, and even decisions under the veil of Harem. These women, apart from having political knowledge, also had a taste in writing and literature. They were fond of poems and verses. Royal women were provided education from the very beginning. There were special arrangements that were made by the nobles to ensure their learning.

Akbar, as an emperor, made provisions for the education of women in the harem. This signifies the importance that was given to women in the field of knowledge.

There were ladies who were assigned the task of educating the daughters of the emperors. From a young age, they were made aware of the politics, economics, and overall functioning of the empire. Many women used to develop an interest in writing poetry and verses as they grew up.

Image- Zeb-un-Nissa
Photo Source- Wikipedia

In the Mughal times, even though they were allowed to read and write, there used to be certain restrictions in terms of the content they could put out. Women were supposed to write on general themes, and any topic that was against the Mughal authority was prohibited.

But these restrictions couldn't keep the women caged. They found a way for themselves. They knew that they wanted to express their feelings, be it love or rage. Amid all the restrictions on their writings, came Makhfi, a pen name that means 'hidden' or 'concealed'. This pen name gave the women new wings and helped them soar to heights in the field of literacy. It was because of this pen name that they were able to express their emotions, and these writings continue to be a window for contemporary historians to peek into the historical times.

We find many examples of the women who wrote under the pen name of Makhfi. The foremost example is of Zeb-un-Nissa. She was the eldest child of Aurengzeb, an orthodox ruler who wasn't in support of any art form. Aurengzed appointed Hafiza Mariam, a woman of the court, to educate her daughter. It is said that Zeb-un-Nissa acquired the taste of learning and knowledge from her father.

As she grew up, Zeb-un-Nissa became a patron of art and calligraphy and was also a collector of manuscripts. Being a spiritual lady, she had a deep knowledge of the verses of the Quran, but her spiritual sense was non-conventional, with liberal thoughts possessing a stark contrast with those of her father's. She even used to engage in 'Mushairas', which were poetic tournaments, but her greatest achievement was in the sphere of literacy.

She was a quick learner and even became a Hafiza at the age of seven. As she grew up, she wrote many books under the pen name of Makhfi. The reason behind choosing a pen name was to prevent herself from being noticed. Her father, who was an orthodox leader, even imprisoned her in the last 20 years of her life because of her writings as a poet.

Zeb-un-Nissa spent all her life on literary works and poetry, as she herself said:

Oh Makhfi, it is the path of love, and alone you must go.

No one suits your friendship, even if God be, though.

Another reason, which is why she wrote as Makhfi, was her fondness towards Sufism, a mystical branch of Islam. Sufi views had been a great force of attraction for her, but because of the more liberal views and practices, Aurengzeb was against it. It is believed that she used her pen name to shield her views and beliefs from her father. Even after knowing the consequences, Zeb-un-Nissa went a step forward when she wrote Diwan-i-Makhfi, which describes her life and even the beauty of Sufi views.

While Zeb-un-Nissa is a highlighted example under the pen name Makhfi, she wasn't the only Mughal lady to do so. Salime Sultan Begum, the niece of Emperor Humayun, was well versed in Persian and possessed a great taste in literacy. After the death of her husband Bairam Khan, she was married to Akbar. In her works, she also used the pen name Makhfi. She made a rich contribution in the field of literacy and even possessed a library of her own at that time. Noor Jhan was another example of a woman who wrote under the pen name Makhfi, the concealed one.

Despite the restrictions and constraints that were placed on the writings of women, they found a way for themselves. They wanted to express their feelings and emotions, to which they forged a solution as Makhfi. It was more than a pen name; it was their identity; it was the mark of their freedom of thoughts and speech in a world that was male-dominated. It was their legacy and heritage that was continued by women in the future.

Such were the women of Medieval India, who stood up for themselves and made their own way amid all the odds.

## Angiya Kurti - More Than A Garment

Mughal women had contributed greatly in the domain of architecture and designs. We find mention of many queens, both in domestic and written records of foreign travelers, who had greatly patronized architecture in that time. Nur Jahn is a classic example here. The women who commissioned a large number of monuments, which the contemporary world proudly owns as its heritage.

Apart from their contribution in the domain of architecture, they were also involved in styling and fashion. The royal queens at that time had certain privileges as compared to the rest of the women in the society. They were given the window to educate themselves; they used to play a role in politics and more. But it was also about wearing heavy clothes, which even created a hindrance to their free movement. It was a difficult task to move in that multilayered garment. It was a problem that they never highlighted, probably because they were used to it, but it was solved by the coming of Angiya Kurti.

The credit for the emergence of Angiya Kurti is given to Zeb-un-Nissa, the eldest daughter of Aurengzeb. She was the one who revolutionized the fashion of Mughal women and brought in a more comfortable design for them. For us, it might look like a choice made for comfort, but for the women back then, it was a sign of empowerment.

The decision to shift from traditional attire to a more contemporary aesthetic and comfortable garment was a sign of their individuality. We are talking about the time when the purdah system was prevalent, where women were considered inferior, and where society was dominated by males. It was in that society that Angiya Kurti was welcomed and accepted by both the royal women and the common ones too.

The Angiya Kurti was a more relaxed and practical garment with more elegance along with comfort, which allowed women more free movement instead of the earlier restricted movement. They felt more confident in a garment that was designed by a woman for women.

Medieval India had seen oppression of women and their rights being crushed. The time was such that they had to stand up for themselves and for their rights. In such a time, Angiya Kurti came as motivation for women. It was a piece of garment, but it broke the chain of wearing tedious attire. It was the liberation of women from an uncomfortable garment, but for them, it was also a step towards establishing their identity. It was a move in the direction to assert their individualism.

Apart from being a piece of garment, it was a canvas for the females. With the intricate designs weaved on the Angiya Kurti, the choice of vibrant colors that were made, and the patterns that were printed, they all came as an expression of the female in the society. The cultural shifts of that time were reflected in the Angiya Kurti, which was also a mirror for the cultural society. With the more vibrant colors in use, it was a sign that women were determined to be more present and visible in the Mughal court and the overall society. It was an expression of their rights and their presence. It was a reflection of the shifts that were taking place in the mindset of the women in society.

A wide acceptance was given to Angiya Kurti by the women. It was from them a realization of their capabilities and the fact that they can make their own decision for their comfort. It was more than a garment for them; it was a sense of freedom from the imposed rules.

## Uncaging The Rights With Spiritualism

The Bhakti movement, which emerged in medieval India, has been seen as a pivotal socio-religious reform movement in the history of our country. It was a result of oppressive religious practices and rituals that were increasing the dominance of the caste system. The rigorous form of caste system, just like the ostracization of women, too emerged from the misinterpretation of our ancient texts. The rigid caste hierarchies distorted their original values of unity and spiritual equality found in Hinduism. Bhakti saints emphasized devotion over ritual, challenging these divisive norms by promoting an inclusive, accessible path to spirituality that transcended caste and gender barriers, paving the way for social unity.

Image- MirabaiImage
Source- Wikipedia

The Bhakti movement provided the platform for people of all castes and genders to become a part of change.

The society before the emergence of the Bhakti Movement was highly oppressive, especially against the women and the lower castes. With the emergence of the movement came reforms that helped the depressed and people of the lower rungs of Indian society.

The Bhakti movement has been seen as a major reform that emphasized the emotion of devotion in people towards the Lord irrespective of their caste. As a result, society saw the emergence of many saints and poets who wrote devotional music together and played an important role in weakening the well-established caste hierarchy.

The movement had no boundaries in terms of caste and gender. As a result, women of medieval India emerged as saints and played their role in the movement. They stood against the odds that prevailed in society and even broke the bondages of households by becoming saints. We have many examples of women saints from the Bhakti movement, but Mirabai is a well-known personality. She has been personified as a devotional poet, but it was she who stood up for herself and even challenged the norms of the patriarchal society.

Mirabai, known for the composition of many bhajans and her devotion towards Lord Krishna. But little is known about her challenging behavior and how she questioned the status quo of society and even shook the social order of that time by making contrasting choices from the prevalent norms.

For instance, Mirabai was married to Raja Bhojraj, and after his death she was expected to commit sati by the members of the society. She was a Rajput wife, and sati was a norm for them, but she committed a powerful assault on the patriarchal expectations by declaring **"sati na hosya,"** which means "I shall not commit sati." Her decision came as an attack on the notion of 'patiparmeshvar' as per which husband is the god for wife and she should be devoted to him and thereby should live and die with him. Her decisions signified that she had the right to live and that her life was not the slave of societal norms. Her decision to say no to sati put the males of society in an uncomfortable situation. It was Mirabia who stood as a pillar of strength for herself.

Another decision that tremendously affected the established norms of that time by the bhakti saint was her choice of Guru. In a caste-ridden society, royal women were bound to be the students of upper-caste gurus. Any decision otherwise was considered unacceptable. Mirabai, being the saint, chose Ravidas, a low-caste saint poet, as her guru. This decision of Mirabai, the princess of Mewar, was not compatible with societal standards. But because Mirabai was a Bhakti saint, she had no caste-based boundations in her spiritual journey. This bold move by the female saint was again seen as a strong rebellion against the acceptable standards.

Mirabai was a strong devotee of Lord Krishna. She even used to meet and interact with bhakts and saints irrespective of their caste and gender. She used to sing and dance in between the Krishna bhakts, and this was her way of defying her identity as a princess and her rejection of all the rigid social expectations.

With the emergence of the Bhakti movement, the devotional aspect came into the picture, which was distinct from the traditional culture. It allowed the dissolution of the caste hierarchy and a culture free of gender distinction. Women of that time used to mobilize to ignite the importance of their rights. They dwelled in devotion, but they also acquired the sense of liberty of their thoughts, choices, and decisions. Mirabai, who opposed the male-dominated culture in almost every aspect, is a great example of how women made their own path leading to their liberation via devotional means. Their hymns and poems were about love, equality, and peace as well. Their journey on spirituality made them bring a sense of individualism and power in them.

All those women who were part of the Bhakti Movement took up attributes that were historically ceded to males. They even cast a shadow on the words of Manu, which were against women. They finally acknowledged their individualism and kept moving for their rights in society. The movement, which was spiritualistic in nature, was used by women to express their rights in the form of poetry and even bhajans.

Apart from Mirabai, the Bhakti Movement also saw the involvement of other women saints such as Akkamahadevi, Janabai, Karaikkal Ammaiyal, Andal, the only female Alwar saint, and more.

The domain of spiritualism, where these women devoted themselves to the almighty, also used the stage for raising their rights. They broke many norms and took steps that were unacceptable as per society, but they stood firm. These women devotees utilized the path of spiritualism to express their vision and to gain their rights.

# CHAPTER 10

# Women of South India

The status of women in medieval India is often portrayed negatively, yet there are notable examples of cultures and dynasties where women held significant power. Some kingdoms were matrilineal, allowing women to inherit and rule. In many cases, these queens emerged as strong leaders in a predominantly male society.

In southern India, especially, there were kingdoms that thrived under the leadership of capable women. These queens not only governed effectively but also demonstrated their strength and intelligence in navigating political challenges. Some women were given the opportunity to rule, while others forged their own paths to leadership, proving their worth in a society that often underestimated them.

These women did not shy away from defending their realms. Many bravely fought against British colonial forces and their oppressive policies. They refused to conform to the norms of a male-dominated empire and actively shaped their destinies, becoming not just rulers but fierce warriors. The stories of these women highlight a rich but often overlooked history of female leadership in medieval India.

Let us take a look at some examples of women rulers and their empires -

## The Kakatiya Dynasty

It was one of those few dynasties that were ruled by women rulers in southern medieval India. Rudrama Devi was the only female ruler in the dynasty and had the courage to come to the throne in a male-dominated society.

She had to prove her capabilities, and even after that, she adopted a masculine name and wore the clothes that were generally associated with the males of the society. She adapted a male persona in a society where women were excluded and considered inferior. Rudrama was a ruler with

Image- Rudrana DeviImage
Source- Go Heritage Run

brains. She possessed the capabilities of swiftly navigating through a complex political landscape, had a stronghold in forging alliances, and even ebbed her enemies. Apart from that, she was a great patron of art and architecture as well. Some of her architectural marvels continue to stand even today. She was a woman who stood up as an inspiration in a male-dominated society and broke the evil of glass- ceilings and gender stereotyping in that era. She was a smart lady and emerged as a learned and capable ruler of her time.

## The Chalukyas Of Kalyana

The Chalukya dynasty saw a number of women rulers during its time who were well versed in political knowledge and were potent and capable. These women had strong personalities and ruled over a large area. Some of the queens from the dynasty are Kaitaladevi, Mailaladevi, Lachchalamahadev,

Lakshmidevi, Savaladevi, Suggaladevi, Kundamarasa, and Akkadevi.

Akkadevi had been a celebrated name in the dynasty as she had ruled on villages such as Pannaleyakote, Kisukadu, Tagare, and Masavadi. She even finds her mention in an inscription that says:

**Ari-nripa-mukuta ghatita-charanaravimdeyar Gamga-sanana pavitreyar-ddin-a natha Chintamanigal eka vakyeyar-ggunada Bedamagiyar appa srimad Akkadeviyar.**

This inscription highlights her familiarity with the science of warfare, and she even seemed to have a council of ministers composed of seven ministers.

## The Queen Of Kittur

Rani Chnnamma was born in the village of Kakati, which is in today's Karnataka. She was married to Raja Mallasaraja of the Desai family and became the queen of Kittur. After the death of her son, she adopted another child, but with the Doctrine of Lapse, the kingdom had no legal heir, and as a result, it was to be annexed by the British East India Company. Brave Rani Chennamma stood fiercely against the power that had a hold over most of the Indian territory. She stood up against the force in front of which even the male-ruled kingdoms had surrendered. The Queen of Kittur was an inspiration to many women of that time as she fought battles against the Britishers without fearing for her life to protect the sovereignty of her kingdom.

The charisma and bravery of the queen had been cherished by many. As a tribute to the brave queen, the Government of India, in the year 2007, unveiled the statue of Rani

Chennamma of Kittur in the Parliament complex in New Delhi, and the unveiling was itself done by the first woman president of India, Smt. Pratibha Devisingh Patil.

Image- Rani Chennamma
Image Source- Wikipedia

We find the mention of these rulers in many historic texts and even in those that were documented by the foreign travelers like Domingo Paes and Nuniz. They traveled in southern India and mentioned the women as learned beings and how they even took part in writing accounts of the kingdom.

There were many more examples of women who were on their feet when it came to expressing their courage and bravery in society. Priyaketaladevi, queen of Chalukya Vikramaditya, and Jakkiabbe, a ruler who ruled over seventy villages, are other examples. They were the ones who didn't allow the community to guide them; they instead believed in being their own boss. They made their own decisions and formed their own blueprints for life.

# CHAPTER 11

## A New Dawn Of Empowerment

Modern India witnessed the coming of the British forces on the land of the Indian subcontinent. These foreign forces brought with them new changes and norms. Britishers ruled India through the East India company. The company was attracted by the resources of the subcontinent and initially had no intent of establishing an administrative base. Later, the declining power of the Mughal Empire and the void created by their absence provided them a window to see themselves as the new rulers.

With time, European forces like the British, French, Spanish, and Dutch fought amongst themselves to establish their hegemony on trade. India, as a result, saw many blood-shedding wars, and after all the battles, British forces emerged as the supreme leader.

The dawn of modern India brought with it a wave of social, political, and cultural change, laying the groundwork for women's empowerment in ways previously unimaginable. For centuries, Indian women had been relegated to the periphery, confined by patriarchal norms and societal expectations. However, the early 20th century marked a transformative period as women began to emerge from the shadows, raising their voices against oppression and asserting their rights in the public sphere.

During this era, India was grappling with the dual forces of colonialism and its own deeply entrenched social hierarchies. Amid the struggle for independence, women found themselves at the crossroads of a larger revolution—not just for political freedom, but for gender equality. While the country fought for sovereignty, women formed their own organizations, established associations, and began to lead movements aimed at securing rights in education, marriage, inheritance, and social welfare. These efforts culminated in a collective push to reform the laws and practices that had long marginalized them.

It was within this climate of reform and activism that women from different regions, religions, and social backgrounds began to unite, forming associations dedicated to changing the status of women in India. Their collective efforts in lobbying for change brought about landmark legislation such as the Hindu Women's Right to Property Act of 1939 and the Child Marriage Restraint Act of 1929, symbolizing the first major legal victories in the fight for women's rights.

Through education, leadership, and social reforms, women in modern India sought not only to uplift themselves but also to reshape the future for generations to come. We can notice something very interesting here as well, it was during this time that the idea of women empowerment somewhere started reaching the masses. The chapter that follows delves into the significant associations and the fearless women who spearheaded this movement, carving out a space for themselves in India's evolving social landscape.

## Associations In Modern India

In modern India, women started participating in politics and social upliftment. They became the voice for their own selves. From participating in revolts, strikes to participating in the freedom struggle, to raising voice against the injustices, the modern era saw the rise of women as a section of society. From a few names of empowered women, the recent decades saw the rise of women in general. The struggles in the past were multifaceted, dealing with different sets of problems that emerged due to the British's unjustified rules. There were people from around the subcontinent that were taking part in these revolts in order to get their sovereignty back.

These revolts saw the coming of many associations, which gave us many prominent leaders on the national stage.

These associations were generally working for a particular cause, some for particular rights, but there were many that were playing their role in different areas. That era also saw the coming of females who formed their own associations and led them. These females were dedicated to bringing about change in the situation of women of the time who had been suppressed by societal norms. There were associations that were built by the females for the females and used the platform to highlight their needs and demands.

We have many examples of such associations. Let's know about them one by one.

## All India Women's Conference

One of the oldest associations formed for the rights of women, the idea was given by Irish-born theosophists, the Margret Cousins, in 1926. It was an association that was concerned with the rights of women in education, social welfare, and even in the domain of marriage and inheritance.

The year 1927 saw the first meeting of the All India Women's Conference in Poona. It was called by Margret Cousins, who were concerned about the issues of women's education in India. All the delegates from different parts of the country came to attend the first official meeting. They were from different regions and castes, and the country saw the first ever association of women belonging to different sections.

The first meeting saw the discussion of problems that were existing, and many resolutions were passed to solve them. These resolutions were about primary education and college-level programs. Women of the conference worked together and kept moving in the direction of upliftment of women in society.

Later, they even expanded the scope of their work and included the discussion on many other problems that were existing. As a result, they involved a social reform agenda. The members of the organization began their involvement in the legislative sphere in order to combat the problems of child marriage as well as women's rights to marriage and divorce.

It was the time when society was witnessing the uprising of many groups and the counter-uprising of British oppressive rules to ground the growing revolts. Amid all the protests, the association decided to get directly involved in creating change. They used different strategies, beginning from campaigns to leadership training. Members of the association worked on issues such as health and family welfare, including women's labor and their trafficking. They even began microcredit programs for women and provided them training in the spectrum of fields and textiles and ensured their employment. This move was to make women economically independent.

All the efforts of the association didn't go in vain. Their meeting and decisions bore fruit. They were in some way part of the overall change that took place. They played a crucial role in making people aware and women empowered. With the combined efforts of many liberal social reformers and the overall effects of these working groups the Hindu Women's Right to Property Act was passed in 1939. Apart from this, the Child Marriage Restraint Act of 1929 was also passed. These two laws were aimed at empowering women and improving their situation in society.

## Women's India Association

It was an important organization that started in 1917 in Adyar, Madras. The organization was founded by women such as Annie Besant, Margaret Cousins, and Dorothy Jinarajadasa. It was the first organization that created an overall awakening among women. The organization was involved in influencing government policies on subjects like women's suffrage, education, and social reforms. It also supported the primary education of girls and described themselves as "Daughters of India.".

The organization gained prominence, and it expanded in different states. The Women's Indian Association, which started in 1917, had 43 branches in 1922 with 2300 members.

## National Council Of Women In India

The National Council of Women in India was founded in 1925 and came to be accepted as a branch of the International Council of Women. As a result, it became the first women's organization in India that was associated with an international organization. The association was provided an opportunity by the President of the International Council of Women to join them. This invitation was seen as an opportunity by the members to raise their voice on an international platform.

The presidency of the council was taken by different women at different times. The Maharani of Baroda took the charge till 1928, and later, from 938–1944, Maharani Setu Parvati Bai of Travancore was President. Another key figure in the council was the chairperson of the executive committee of the Bombay Council, Meherbai Tata.

These were some of the examples of the associations that were formed by women and dealt with the problems that were faced by women. Many of them played a crucial role in crafting many laws that uplifted the status of women in society. It was the hard work and dedication of these associations that the society witnessed legal actions against women's oppression.

## Literature

With the increasing demand for rights and the confidence of women because of their association with different groups, it was helping them to break the cage of restrictions and make themselves free. But the groups and associations were not in the reach of each and every female in the society. As a result, women found another way to reach the untouched sections and the women there.

In order to make the idea of liberation and rights reach every woman, the use of printed material began. Newspapers and magazines were initiated by many women organizations who were aiming to tap the women in the lower strata who were not able to be involved in the women groups.

These newspapers and journals dealt with a variety of issues and helped in providing insight to these women of what was happening around them and in other states and even made them aware about their rights and liberties.

Historical evidence has provided us with information about many of these literary sources.

Stri Dharma was one such monthly journal that evolved at the time when Swaraj was the motto. The title Stri Dharma means the duties of women or justice for women. This journal was launched by Margaret cousins. Later, Dr.

Muthulakshmi Reddy became the editor of this magazine, along with holding the position of first woman legislature in British India.

The journal was published from 1918–1936. It was multilingual, with portions of Hindu, Tamil, and Telugu. This journal was used by Indian women to give the women's movement a voice.

A major periodical of the 20th century, it was published in Hindi by a prominent feminist of that time, Kamladevi Chattopadhyaya, along with others. It was a monthly publication with its major objective being educating the people. It used to highlight the problems being faced by women. It also discussed the policies that were being carried out at that time and their effect on the females of the society. It emerged as a platform that offered a dialogue between advocates and critics of widow remarriage, which was a hot topic of that time.

This monthly used to actively deal with the evils of society. The members of the monthly didn't hesitate to publish about the sensitive topics of marriage rights and enforced widowhood. The members were very vocal about the institution of child marriage.

Child marriage had an impact on the health of the girl child, and therefore this topic was a frequently discussed in Stri-Dharma. It highlighted the physical, mental, and emotional effects that child marriage created. In one of its pages, it described child marriage as "bartering of a girl's liberty."

The changing landscape of the 20th century witnessed the coming of the Sharda Act in 1929. It was a law that set the minimum age limit for boys and girls to get married. The journal played an active role in the aftermath of the law. It discussed the pros and cons along with the shortcomings of the law.

Another issue that Stri-Dharma dealt with was divorce. There were articles that talked about the impartiality between men and women for marriage and divorce. The contributors of Stri-Dharma therefore highlighted the Hindu Marriage Dissolution Bill, which was passed in British India. They unveiled the lackings in the legislature. They published many articles that were to make women aware of the impact of the bill on their lives.

The Deshmukh bill, also known as the Hindu Women's Right to Property Act of 1937, also saw a discussion in the pages of Stri-Dharma. It argued the bill to be "only a case of restoration of the lost rights to Hindu women."

The monthly at that time was seen as a pivotal literary source by the women of that time. It was consumed by both genders and made the plight of the women come in front of society. The articles were educational in nature. They used to discuss the major bills dealing with women's rights and used to explain their impact on the lives of the women of that time.

Arya Mahila was another journal edited by Sanatan Dharma Mahamandal that looked at the status of women on the basis of the Vedic knowledge.

Another example is the Ghara Jeuti magazine. It was the first women's magazine that was published in 1927. This was seen as a true women's journal because before it, a very few women were involved in the literary domain. The magazine saw the articles by radical women such as Puspalata Das and Swarnalata Saikiani. They talked about the women's movement that took place outside Assam. The magazine highlighted the importance of education in the lives of women. There was an article in the magazine by Labanyaprabha Barbora, Stree Sikshar Bishaye Ekakhar (Some notes on women). This article talked about the importance of higher education for women and even emphasized on them for holding a higher degree. Not only that, she even asked the Assamese women to use their skill of weaving as a tool of earning money.

Not only women, the magazine saw the articles by males of the society too who were in favor of women's rights. For example, Taraprasad Chaliha, Durga Prasad Majindar Barua, and Taraunram Phukan. They were in favor of economic freedom for women.

We have different examples of the literary sources that were used by women to empower other women. Bharat Stri Mahamandal's journal and women's era are other examples.

## Tribal Women

As I said, movement had traveled from closed gates to the masses and the ripples were felt in tribes as well. One such ripple gave birth to the story of Rani Gaidinliu.

Rani Gaidinliu, was born on January 26, 1915, in the small village of Luangkao in what is now the Tamenglong district of Manipur. At the tender age of 13, she took her first step into the world of rebellion and reform, joining the Heraka movement, which had been initiated by her cousin, Haipou Jadonoang. The Heraka movement sought to preserve Naga traditions and reject the growing influence of Christian missionaries, and in doing so, it began to challenge the oppressive norms that had subjugated Naga women for generations.

Image- Rani Gaidinliu
Source- PIB

When her cousin was captured and hanged by the British in 1931, many would have expected the movement to die with him. At only 16 years old, she assumed leadership of the movement, carrying its torch. It was during this time that she began preaching Gandhian principles, urging her people to reject British rule by refusing to pay taxes and to refrain from cooperating with colonial authorities.

At 17, Gaidinliu became a revolutionary leader, organizing guerrilla warfare in the Cachar Hills and Hangrum village. These were bold and calculated moves that brought her into direct confrontation with the British. Her bravery and defiance sparked a manhunt, with a bounty placed on her head, but Gaidinliu, undeterred, fought on.

Captured on October 17, 1932, she was sentenced to life imprisonment. The British, unable to break her spirit, hoped to extinguish her influence by locking her away in the prisons of Tura, Guwahati, Shillong, and Aizawl. For

14 years, Gaidinliu remained incarcerated, but her resolve remained unshaken. Even in the depths of the prison cells, her story continued to inspire.

In 1937, Jawaharlal Nehru, upon hearing of her plight, visited her in Shillong jail. Moved by her story, Nehru gave her the title of "Rani," a queen of her people. Yet, despite his support, she was not freed until India gained independence in 1947. But when she emerged from prison, she was more than a mere freedom fighter; she had become a symbol of resistance, a beacon of hope for women across the Naga tribes who had long been marginalized.

Her legacy extended far beyond her fight against the British. Gaidinliu challenged the social fabric of her community, advocating for the rights and dignity of Naga women. In a region where patriarchal norms were deeply embedded, she demonstrated through her leadership that women were not only capable but indispensable in the fight for freedom—both from colonial rule and from oppressive traditions.

Throughout her life, Gaidinliu was honored and celebrated for her bravery and commitment to her people. In 1972, she was awarded the Tamrapatra Freedom Fighter Award, followed by the Padma Bhushan in 1982. Even after her death, in 2015, on her birth centenary, commemorative coins were released in her honor, and in 2016, the Indian Coast Guard commissioned a fast patrol vessel named ICGS Rani Gaidinliu, ensuring that her name continues to sail through history.

## The Unyielding Spirit Of Koya Queen Bângarâ Devi

The Koya Queen, Bângarâ Devi, was a beacon of freedom and a symbol of defiance. Her story begins not with a battlefield, but at the sacred grounds of the Wâlupu festival, where tradition, faith, and identity intertwined for the Koya people. It was during this time that Captain Macneil, an officer of the British Empire, disrupted the sacred Maria sacrifice, an act deeply tied to the spiritual and cultural traditions of the Koya tribe.

This brazen act of colonial arrogance did more than interrupt a festival—it insulted the Koya way of life. Queen Bângarâ Devi felt the insult to her bones. Her pride and her sense of justice would not let the British violation go unanswered. Driven by this deep emotional wound, she began to quietly orchestrate a plan to challenge British dominion over her homeland. Her strategies became the seeds of rebellion, setting in motion a movement that aimed to expel the British from her sacred land.

While Bângarâ Devi battled the British in the forests, Gurubâri Jâni, a woman of quiet strength, was scripting her own chapter in the freedom struggle. She lived in Garudagudâ village, a place nestled in the Nawarangapur district, far from the centers of power, yet alive with the pulse of rebellion together with her husband.

The Jâni couple was united by a singular purpose: freedom from British rule. Gurubâri, however, was not content with merely supporting the movement from the sidelines. She, along with a group of women freedom fighters, embarked on a journey to Sakhigopal, a hub of revolutionary fervor in Puti district, to be trained in the art of struggle. There, these women received education not just in physical combat but in the philosophy of resistance—an education that would arm them for the battles ahead.

Though history has been unkind, often leaving their names in the shadows, Gurubâri Jâni's contribution is impossible to erase. Her courage, her self-sacrifice, and her boldness served as a blueprint for future generations of women to follow, especially in times of national strife. For her, the freedom struggle was not just a battle against the British, but a movement for the dignity and self-respect of her people. Her legacy, like Bângarâ Devi's, was built not on grand titles or wealth but on a relentless commitment to justice.

### Less Known Women Personalities In Indian Freedom Struggle -

#### Rama Devi

Image- Rama Devi Image
Source- Odisha Review

Rama Devi was a prominent freedom fighter and a lady from Orissa. She was born in a wealthy zamindar family but completely abandoned her comforts to fight for the freedom of the nation. She joined the Salt Satyagraha, the Khadi Movement, the Bhoodan and Gramdan Movement, and was imprisoned several times but remained resolute about fighting against the British.

She walked barefoot and traveled all over the state of Orissa organizing meetings for people where she preached M.K. Gandhi's ideals, motivating hundreds of women to take part in the movement. Several women contributed their ornaments, clothes and money, turning the fight into a mass mobilization against colonialism.

Her political career began in 1921, when she and her husband joined the National Congress. Embracing khadi, she met Gandhi in Cuttack that same year, presenting him with a hand-woven cotton bundle as a symbol of her commitment.

In 1930, during the Salt Satyagraha, she played a crucial role in Inchudi and Srijang, where many women joined. She was arrested in November but released after the Gandhi-Irwin Pact. In 1932, after another arrest, she focused on helping Harijans and promoting social reform.

By 1938, she was active in organizing a major meeting with Gandhi and other leaders in Orissa. Following Kasturba Gandhi's death, she became the representative of the Kasturba Trust in the region. During the August Revolution of 1942, she and her family were arrested.

Rama Devi later founded an ashram in Bari, known as Sewaghar, where volunteers engaged in khadi work, education, and community services. She oversaw these efforts personally and dedicated her life to serving the poor and downtrodden, embodying strength and compassion.

## Malati Choudhury

She was born on 26 April 1904 in Patna where her father Kumud Nath Sen, a man from east Bengal who was practicing as a barrister, died when she was only two and a half years old. Malati was reared by her mother Snehlata Sen, who was a writer and a teacher. Her family was rich with politicians but Malati did not choose the path of formal politics. Instead, she decided to work for and with the people.

Image- Malati ChoudhuryImage Source- Ministry of Culture

At the age of 16, she was admitted to ViswaBharati, Santiniketan. Here she was influenced directly by the teachings and principles of Kabindranath Tagore who called her "Minu". Apart from education, she was also learning music and dance. In the process, she acquired knowledge in many performing arts. There she met Nabakrushna Choudhury, the younger son of Gokulanand Choudhury who also came there for education. Both shared each other's thought processes which made them tie the knot in 1927. They settled in a small village Anakhia, in the Jagatsinghpur district, and started community services.

Since she was inspired by Mahatma Gandhi and Rabindranath Tagore in her school days and married Nabakrushna Choudhury who was also from a family of freedom fighters, she dedicated her entire life to the cause of freedom struggle and service of the people. Her journey started in 1930 in Inchudi and then at Kujang, where she motivated hundreds of women to leave their houses and join the Salt Satyagraha. She also inspired other women to picket before the shops selling foreign goods and courted arrest.

In 1942, she carried Gandhi's message 'Do or die' to the people of Odisha and participated in the Quit India Movement for which she was arrested and sentenced to three years imprisonment. After her release, she started the construction of 'Baji Rout Hostel' in Angul where she rehabilitated the tribal and orphan children and taught them. In 1946 she joined Mahatma Gandhi's peace mission in Nuakhali and spent some time there. In 1948, she formed 'Utkal Nabajiban Mandal' for the education of the children of the poor and tribal.

She has won many awards in her life for her contribution to society. But she always raised her voice against injustice for which she and her husband were arrested during an emergency in 1975. She died on 15 March 1998.

## Kuntala Kumari Sabat

She was born on 8 February 1901 in Jagdalpur, Chhattisgarh. Her father, Daniel, a doctor by profession, relocated to Burma later on, but owing to some family complications, Kuntala and her mom had to come back to Odisha. She studied in Khordha and Cuttack and ultimately became a lady doctor herself.

Kuntala equally was an ardent writer contributing to a number of patriotic and revolutionary songs that were prompted by Gopabandhu Das. She wrote in Odia, English, Bengali and Hindi, and fought to bring out the concerns of girls and young women. The motivational poems of such poets as Gandhi and Nehru encouraged many to take part in the fight for independence.

A devoted follower of Gandhi, she believed that independence was every Indian's birthright. Kuntala called on women in Odisha to participate in the movement and advocated for the downtrodden, opposing social inequalities. Notable poems like "Sphuling" and "Ahwan" encourage youth to learn from the past and join the national movement, though some of her works were banned.

Image- Kunatala Kumari Sabat Image Source Ministry of Culture

Kuntala chaired a session of the Utkal Sammilani in Balasore on August 2, 1931. She passed away at 37 in 1938, but her writings left a lasting impact on the fight for independence.

## Sarala Devi

Sarala Devi was born on August 19, 1904, in Narilo village near Balikuda, in what was then the Bengal Presidency. She came from an elite family and was a multifaceted personality—poet, novelist, translator, critic, freedom fighter, feminist, activist, social reformer, and educator. Sarala made significant contributions to modern Odisha and used literature to critique and transform society, advocating for a larger role for women in public life.

Image- Sarala DeviImage
Source- Ministry of Culture

Despite her extensive body of work, much of it has faded from public recognition. However, it's clear that her writings played a vital role in the nationalist movement in Odisha. Sarala Devi, frequently referred to as the Biplababi of Orissa, was detained during her nationalistic endeavors, making her the first Odia woman to be imprisoned for her cause. She was present at the very first political gathering of Odia women only to where Gandhiji spoke on national issues. On April 20, she took part in the Salt Satyagraha at Inchudi, leading the movement alongside prominent figures like Biswanath Das and Niranjan Patnaik.

## Jambubati Pattnaik

Jambubati Devi, a courageous freedom fighter from Western Odisha, was born on November 9, 1886, in Binika village, now in Bargarh district. Even though she had little education, her ability to organize women in Western Odisha to fight for independence was brilliant. It was her husband, Bhagirathi Pattnaik, a freedom fighter himself, who motivated her to act.

Image- Jumbubati PattnaikImage Source- Ministry of Culture

Jambubati's first confrontation with the British occurred in 1930 during the Salt Satyagraha in Balasore, where she was among ten other women fighters. In 1931, she courageously unfurled the national flag in Barpali in spite of threats from the British. Together with her husband, she carried the sidhanta of Gandhi and urged the people to use Swadeshi goods and boycott foreign goods. A large farmers' march was held under her leadership on March 2nd, 1931, and she was arrested with some other workers as a result.

Afterward, she moved to Jharsuguda, where she organized picketing against the sale of foreign liquor, inspiring Harijan women to join the efforts. She was tasked with raising funds for the 'Seva Dal' and training volunteers to promote the freedom struggle among women in Bargarh. Later, she and other freedom fighters went to Cuttack to stage a massive Satyagraha.

On September 22, 1933, Jambubati was arrested again, this time while picketing at a foreign liquor shop in Sambalpur, and spent five months in Bhagalpur jail. As soon as her sentence was served, she engaged in relief work for the earthquake affected regions of Bihar and during that time met with Gandhi and Nehru. On 4 May 1934, she organized Harijans to greet Gandhi at the Jharsuguda railway station. In 1940, the tribal ashram that she built in Amadapada, Ukhrul District, was aimed at providing education to the local tribes and nurturing nationalism. She prepared and trained Congress volunteers who would attend the session in Puri, as a result earned the name 'Ashram Mata'. Her second arrest during the 1938 Satyagraha was in Sambalpur.

During the Quit India Movement in the year 1942 even though her health was deteriorating badly Jambubati besieged the District Court of Dumkar in Bihar along with her family. She was let off in consideration of her medical condition and died while in Bihar on July 7, 1943, having lived a life of exemplary courage and devotion to the cause of freedom struggle.

## Women In Framing The Constitution

Indian land had witnessed many wars and powers. It has seen the Indus Valley civilization, which was followed by the coming up of Arynas, setting up of janapadas and mahajanapadas, which were further replaced by the coming up of Delhi Sultanate. The Sultanate was later overthrown by the Mughals, and during their reign, India witnessed many architectural wonders, which exist even in today's world, reflecting the history that we read in our textbooks. The strong Mughal empire couldn't preserve its glory and rule, and India finally witnessed the rule of Britishers on its soil.

When seen like this, India has been under the rule of foreign powers for a long period of time, and the independence that it gained in 1947 was indeed a hard-earned one. After centuries of cultural and societal evolution, India finally took a deep breath in a free environment on 15th August 1947.

But there were many factors that emerged with time and that were essential for a stable and prospering country that had finally gotten the chance of experiencing its own rules and regulations. Understanding the fragile conditions, steps were taken years before 1947. The forefathers of our independent country knew the essentiality of crafting a document, a coded piece of legislation that would guide the country. It was then that the Constituent Assembly was formed. It was this assembly that was given the task of combining all the pieces of knowledge and experience together and to form a guiding text that would be the source of authority in the coming future.

The members who were given this task composed the constituent assembly. There were many learned people.

Even though the majority of them were male, there were many female members who played their role on equal footing. They were the craftswomen of the independent India; these women were the ones who gained experience and knowledge from their active roles in pre-independent India. These were the women who had been leaders.

Let's introduce ourselves to the framers of the constitution, to the women who crafted the way for the new India.

## 1. Ammu Swaminathan

Ammu Swaminathan was an upper caste Hindu woman born in 1894 in Pallakad, Kerala. She was married to S Swaminathan. It was in the year 1914 that she was drawn towards Indian politics and she wanted to actively be a part of the reformist movements that were going on in the country.

Her intention came into reality when she founded the Women's India Association in 1917 along with other prominent female figures of that time like Kamaladevi Chattopadhyay, Annie Besant and Muthulakshmi Reddy. This association was directly involved in empowering women and to protect their rights.

She joined the Indian National Congress in 1934 and even played an active role in the Quit India Movement. Apart from this, her name is also remembered for her presentation before the Montague Chelmsford Commission and Southborough Commission.

Her journey in the Indian Freedom movement prepared her with the desired skills and abilities for her future endeavors.

Image- Ammu SwaminathanImage
Source- Paper by Bonani Dhar

In 1946, she was elected for the Indian Constituent Assembly from Madras constituency and became one of the few women involved in crafting of the constitution. She was a dedicated woman and actively participated in every debate and meeting of the constituent assembly.

She was in support of women's rights and thereby abided by Dr. B R Ambedkar's principles of equality for the women of the society. Her inclination towards the rights of women can be understood by a section from one of her speeches in which she said, "People outside have been saying that India did not give equal rights to her women. Now we can say that when the Indian people themselves framed their Constitution they have given rights to women equal with every other citizen of the country." From her words, we can understand her vision of creating a country with gender equality and women's rights.

Her role was not limited to the constituent assembly. After independence, she became a member of Lok Sabha in 1952, Rajya Sabha in 1954, became the Vice-President of the Federation of Film Societies and even presided over Bharat Scouts and Guides.

## 2. Dakshayani Velayudhan

Dakshayani Velayudhan was born in 1912 on the island of Bolgatty, Cochin. Born in the Pulaya community, which was a highly discriminated community, Dakshayani was born to break many social norms.

Image- Dakshayani Velayudhan
Image Source- Constitution of India website

As she grew up, she was among the handful of first generation educated people from her community. The community she was born in, women were not allowed to wear an upper garment. They were considered inferior and were highly discriminated against. Dakshayani Velayudhan also became the first woman from her community to wear an upper cloth.

She emerged as a woman with interest in politics and as she grew up, she became a critic of Congress politics. She used many mediums to express her discomfort against Congress. She used All India Scheduled Castes Federation's (AISCF) weekly journal, Jai Bheem, to write her thoughts down.

At the age of 34, she became the first and only dalit woman to be elected in the constituent assembly. She used the opportunity and the platform to express her views and emerged with a strong voice who wasn't afraid to speak against the popular opinion. She expressed her concerns when B.R Ambedkar and M Nagappa came up with the idea of amendment that would require candidates from reserved seats to get a certain percentage of votes from Scheduled Caste voters. She spoke about how it was similar to the concept of separate electorate and was against the idea.

She presented her views on the type of federalism that India should adopt. She even raised her voice against the lack of decentralization which was prevalent in the Draft Constitution of 1948.

After independence, she became part of the provincial parliament and in 1977, she set up a women's rights organization Mahila Jagriti Parishad in Delhi.

To honor her contributions, Kerala Government in 2019 instituted the Dakshayani Velayudhan award for women who were involved in empowerment of other women in the state.

## 3. Begum Aizaz Rasul

Begum Aizaz Rasul was born in 1908 in a princely family in Punjab. She was born in a family which had close association with politics and as a result she developed interest in the political ecosystem at a young age. She even used to accompany her father to political conferences as his assistance. From a very young age she was a critic of oppressive and discriminatory practices and she herself defied the purdah system.

Image- Begum Aizaz Rasul
Image Source- Pleaders

In 1937 she made her debut in electoral politics as a member of UP legislative assembly and served in many important positions like leader of opposition and even as Deputy President of the Council. She emerged as a strong opponent for reservation for minorities and even for the zamindari system.

During the making of the constitution, she represented the Muslim League from the UP constituency. She was the only Muslim woman in the constituent assembly and debated on the topics such as property rights, minority rights, national language, etc.

Rasul was able to continue her political journey even after independence. She was elected to the Rajya Sabha (1952-1956) and was subsequently elected to the legislative assembly of Uttar Pradesh (1969 -1989). Apart from her involvement in the political sphere of independent India, she was also a supporter of women hockey and played an important role in popularizing the sport. She even served as the President of the Indian Women's Hockey Federation for twenty years and then she went on to head the Asian Women's Hockey Federation.

We can understand the importance of thoughts that these women held. They were learned and many had swimmed up in the pool of atrocities and reached the heights where they could express their opinions and problems. There were a total of 15 women in the constituent assembly out of the total 389. These were Ammu Swaminathan, Dakshayani Velayudhan, Begum Aizaz Rasul, Durgabai Deshmukh, Hansa Jivraj Mehta, Kamla Chaudhary, Leela Roy, Malati Choudhury, Purnima Banerjee, Rajkumari Amrit Kaur, Renuka Ray, Sarojini Naidu, Sucheta Kriplani, Vijaya Lakshmi Pandit, and Annie Mascarene

But these handful of women played a crucial role in shaping the constitution, they guided the spirit of the document and made the inclusion and exclusion of many acts and articles. These women presented their views without any fear in the assembly which was dominated by men.

# CHAPTER 12

## Amazing Women Of Modern India

## Dr. Rukhmabai

Rukmabai Raut was born on November 22, 1864, in Mumbai, India, into a Brahmin family, where her father, Janardhan Pandurang, a scholar, instilled in her a passion for education despite the restrictive societal norms of the time. Her journey toward independence and education was marked by significant challenges, particularly concerning her early marriage.

Image- Dr. Rukhmabai
Source- feminismindia.com

At the age of 11, Rukmabai was forcefully married to Dadaji Bhikaji, a man much older than her, in 1875. As she matured, Rukmabai came to understand her rights and boldly refused to live with her husband, a decision that led to the famous "Rukmabai Case." This legal battle, which sought to nullify her marriage, sparked a nationwide debate on women's rights and marriage practices in colonial India. Though initially losing the case, Rukmabai's determination set a precedent. In one account, it is suggested that Queen Victoria intervened, dissolving the marriage. However, another widely accepted version indicates that Bhikaji agreed to dissolve the marriage for a sum of two thousand rupees in 1888.

Freed from the constraints of her unwanted marriage, Rukmabai pursued her passion for medicine, supported by progressive leaders and her family. She traveled to England and became the first Indian woman to study medicine, earning her degree from the London School of Medicine for Women. This achievement was groundbreaking in a time when Indian women were often denied access to education, particularly in male-dominated fields like medicine.

After a long and successful career, Rukmabai continued to advocate for women's rights, even publishing a pamphlet titled "Purdah: The Need for its Abolition" in 1929, where she argued for the rights of young widows to contribute meaningfully to society. Rukmabai's legacy, culminating in her death in 1955, stands as a testament to her fight for gender equality and social justice. Her life story is celebrated in modern times, including through the Marathi biopic Doctor Rakhmabai, released in 2016.

## Tarabai Shinde

By the 19th century, women were denied basic rights, particularly education. Tarabai Shinde, a pioneering feminist from Maharashtra, challenged these limitations. Though she did not receive formal schooling, she was educated by her father, Bapuji Hari Shinde, and became a voracious reader. Despite societal customs, she chose a nontraditional life, remaining childless and having her husband live in her household—an unusual arrangement in a patriarchal society.

Shinde's groundbreaking work, Stri Purush Tulana (1882), criticized both caste and patriarchy, becoming one of the earliest modern Indian feminist texts. In it, she questioned the legitimacy of patriarchal norms upheld by religious texts

Image- Tarabai Shinde
Image Source- IMPR

and condemned the oppression of women. Her critiques were daring and provocative, particularly in a society that refused to recognize women's autonomy.

In addition to her literary contributions, Shinde was an active member of the Satyashodhak Samaj, a social reform movement founded by Jyotirao Phule. This movement challenged caste and gender inequalities, including efforts to educate women and provide refuge for upper-caste widows. Shinde's activism was a precursor to later feminist movements, inspiring generations of women to question entrenched systems of oppression.

Despite progress in some areas, gender inequality persists. Even today, girls are often seen as less desirable than boys, leading to practices like female infanticide, particularly in parts of Madhya Pradesh and Rajasthan. While men may possess greater physical strength, women make up almost half the population and are essential to family and societal life. Ironically, those who devalue women forget that they rely on women to birth the very male heirs they prize.

Women's contributions are undervalued both at home, where they perform unpaid labor, and in the larger social context. Yet, their potential role in national development is undeniable. To truly become a developed nation, as envisioned in the concept of Viksit Bharat, India must address these deep-rooted issues and promote gender equality.

In recent years, the Indian government has launched various initiatives to empower women and improve their social, educational, and economic standing. The National Education Policy (NEP) 2020 emphasizes gender equity, aiming to provide equal access to education for all. Vocational training programs and the Skill India Mission are also designed to enhance women's economic independence.

Additional programs such as **Pradhan Mantri Ujjwala Yojana** (providing clean cooking fuel), Beti Bachao, Beti Padhao (encouraging the education and protection of girls), and **Pradhan Mantri Mudra Yojana** (supporting women entrepreneurs) represent steps towards a more inclusive society. Efforts under the Nirbhaya Fund, including Safe City Projects and Fast Track Special Courts, address violence against women and aim to create safer environments for them.

Despite these positive initiatives, significant challenges

remain. Deeply entrenched social stigmas continue to devalue women's contributions, and gender inequality persists in all sectors. Violence against women—domestic violence, sexual assault, and human trafficking—remains rampant. These issues, exacerbated by a lack of safe spaces, prevent women from achieving their full potential.

Additionally, women face barriers to economic participation. Wage disparities, limited career advancement, and the challenges of balancing work and family responsibilities hinder their progress. While policies for maternity leave exist, they are not universally effective, and more support is needed to ensure women can thrive in the workforce.

Tarabai Shinde's fearless advocacy for women's rights remains a guiding light in the struggle for gender equality. Her critique of oppressive social norms was ahead of its time, and her legacy continues to inspire feminists today. Yet, as India strives to meet Sustainable Development Goal (SDG) 5—achieving gender equality and empowering all women and girls—there is much work to be done.

## Pandita Ramabai

Pandita Ramabai was born on April 23, 1858, into a Brahmin family in India. In the era she was born in, education for women was not even in the picture. People used to consider females better off without academic learning. In that era, Ramabai emerged as a learned child One who was proficient in Sanskrit. All thanks to her father, Ananta Shastri, who was a scholar and thought of knowledge as a gender-neutral requirement.

It was Anant Shashtri who believed that knowledge was an excellent thing. He wanted to surpass his intellect

Image- Pandita Ramabai
Image Source- Indian liberals

for his wife and daughter. But the society was cruel. He faced continuous oppression, but he was firm. To ensure the education of his wife and daughter, he left his town and settled in the forest with his family. He took care of his family but sedulously taught them Sanskrit. Time was tough; they had to begin from scratch. To make it worse, the devastating famine of 1876–78 came. Famine caused them a hard time. Ramabai's family had nothing to eat. In the book "PANDITA RAMABAI: The Story of Her Life" by Helen S. Dyer, the author has mentioned how Ramabai had to rely on the mercy of others. She even begged for food but still couldn't save her father and mother from dying out of starvation.

Ramabai was 16 when she lost both her parents. In a world that was grappling with famine, she was left with her brother to survive. The situations were cruel; food was scarce. To search for a better life, Ramabai and her brother moved to Northern India. Ramabi was a fighter. She had seen days when her brother was earning four rupees per month and they couldn't afford three meals. While wandering, Ramabai had access to homes of high-caste Hindus. This made her aware of the situations of women. She became familiar with the reality of society and resolved to devote her life to the upliftment of unfortunate women, especially childwidows.

From sleeping on the roadside to searching for work, the siblings reached Calcutta. It was here that her firmness in Sanskrit was recognized by the University of Calcutta, and she was bestowed with the title of 'Pundita'. It was big news at that time and reached the ears of many big personalities. From here, Ramabai and her brother got involved in public lectures dealing with the cause of education for women. Years later, Ramabai lost her only family, her brother, to illness.

In 1880, Ramabai made a bold decision. She got married to Bipin Behari Medhvi. He was a lawyer and belonged to a different caste. This decision was a direct challenge to the norms of society. She was living a happy life until, in 1882, she lost her husband too. In a world that was cruel to widows, Ramabai was left with her only daughter, Manoramabai.

Ramabai lost her parents, her brother, and then her husband. But her determination to work for the education of women was unshaken. To accomplish her mission, she left for Puna with her daughter. She resumed her former occupation as a lecturer there.

Ramabai noticed an anomaly in Poona and North-West provinces. The gap between the status of women and widows was wide. In Poona, where females were allowed to express themselves, they were cages within the four walls in Northern India. Women in Bobay were allowed to be seen and to be expressed. Ramabai picked the opportunity, and with her knowledge of Shashtras and teachings, she began preaching instructions to women about education and child marriage.

Ramabai's lectures grasped the vision of high-class families in Poona. They were impressed by the work of Ramabai. Ramabai nudged the confidence in forming a society of high-class women. The aim was to educate women, and it manifested itself in the form of Aarya Mahila Samaj. It was the first step that Ramabai took to accomplish her dream.

Ramabai was passionate about education. Just like her father, she believed it to be pivotal for women. Arya Mahila Samaja provided her a platform with masses to express her concerns and beliefs. In 1882, Hunter Omission had landed in India. It was a move by the British Government to look into the matter of education. When the commission came to Poona, Ramabai became the face of the Aarya Mahila Samaj and presented her views. She talked about the training of the teachers and admitting women to medical colleges. Her ideas were so influential that they even reached Queen Victoria, proving her voice mattered in a time when women were often overlooked.

Ramabai kept working towards the educational rights of the women. In 1883, driven by her ambition to become a doctor, Ramabai traveled to Britain. This journey was challenging, but she was determined. In England, she was keenly welcomed by the England Sisterhood at Wantage. There were many hurdles that Ramabai faced on foreign soil while pursuing her education.

She remembered how in Calcutta she made her first acquaintance with the Christian Scripture. She was having time in her hand and decided to continue her exploration of the religion. It was at this point that Ramabai, along with her daughter, got baptized—a significant step that reflected her free spirit. She was a woman who kept her thinking open-ended and looked at things through a different lens, a lens not known to the common society. Her religious conversion was a bold step, which signified that she had an uncaged personality. Her zeal for bringing about the change she wanted to see is reflected in her baptism move. But she was aware of her goal, her motto of working for the education of women. Baptism could have brought her a backlash from the Hindus of society. Keeping the possibility in mind, she kept her food habits intact. She didn't let the conversion change her completely as a human. It was also an attempt by Ramabai to showcase that conversions need not necessarily mean a reversal in belief systems.

Ramabai received a call from Cheltenham Ladies' College after spending a year in Wantage. She found it to be her chance of studying mathematics, natural science, and English literature. After 1.5 years of being in Chelsea, she got an invitation from the USA. The invite was from Anandibai Joshi, who was a student at the Women's Medical College of Philadelphia. She wanted Ramabi to witness her graduation ceremony.

Initially concerned about her own education, reluctant Ramabai ended up staying three years in the USA. She used the time to deliver lectures and even translate books. Her interaction with a new sphere of people made her idea more profound. Alongside her daily works, she wrote her very popular book at this time, "The High-Caste Hindu Woman."

The book unfolded the harsh conditions of women in British India. It was a window for the outside world to peek into the realities of India's female lives. In the preface of the book, Dr. Bodley, an American woman who supported Ramabai, aptly said, "The silence of a thousand years has been broken!". This signifies the importance that the book held at that time. It was a voice given to all the helpless females of Indian society.

Ramabai formed many circles of people with a similar mindset.

In 1888, Ramabai returned to India and committed herself to social work. She gathered the funds from her local supporters and international friends to inaugurate Shardas Sadan. It was a dream come true. Sarada Sadan was a home for widows, which gained immense popularity within a fraction of time. It began with two pupils, which then grew to 350. This Sadan was more than a widow home for the women. It was a place where marginalized females found a new identity.

Ramabai, driven by her passion for education, provided educational support to the members of the Sadan. It was her efforts that gave these women the hope for living a dignified life. She made them self-aware, aware about their rights and opportunities as well.

Her vision was not aligned with that of the conservative section of society. She faced backlashes from some but also gained support and admiration from others. During the 1890's, famine hit the country. At that time, Ramabai relocated women and children. She helped the underprivileged and worst-affected sections of society by her Mukti Mission. Her mission not only provided the outcast children and underprivileged women a shelter but also a sense of belonging.

Pandita Ramabai's life was filled with resilience and determination. She wasn't only a thinker; she was a personality who put actions to her thoughts. She was a firm supporter of women's education and their rights. She played a pivotal role for women's empowerment during an era that was eclipsed by patriarchy. In a world where change was difficult, Ramabai reminded the women that determination can lead to achievements, no matter the situation. Her legacy continues to inspire women even today. Her story is a reminder for standing up against injustice and to support what is right.

## Priya Jhingam

Born on December 25, 1939, in a traditional family in India, Priya Jhingam was the first lady officer of the Indian Army. She is the perfect example of the saying, 'Where there is a will, there is a way.'

Image- Priya Jhingham

Image Source- majorpriyajhingham.com

Priya Jingham completed her higher education from Lady Shri Ram College in Delhi. When she was growing up, she always wanted to serve the country, one way or another. Her father was a police officer; the exposure she got with him provided her the grounds to think of aspiring to become the same. Army was not an option because, back then, women officers were not allowed in the defense. But Priya was determined, and she wrote a letter to then Chief of Army Staff, General Sunith Francis Rodrigues. She, in her letter, requested that he open the doors of the defense for women. She didn't know whether the letter had reached the chief or not and had little hope of getting a reply. But one day, she witnessed the highest moment of her life. It was the reply to her letter. The Chief wrote back a personal reply to her, and it was a signed letter stating that within a year or two, women would be welcomed in the defense services.

Priya was on cloud nine, and she immediately began to prepare for her selection. In the meantime, she decided to study law. In the year 1992, the defense services finally rolled out the official notification for the admission of women candidates in the defense services. There was a quota for 2 seats under the law category, and Priya was determined to bag one. She was extremely confident about her selection, which is evident from her words: "There were two seats reserved for law graduates. I was just curious to find out who the other person might be." Her confidence was a result of her dedication. She had waited for this moment for a long period of time.

In 1993, her words were proved right, and she was inducted by the Indian army in their first batch, after which she left for OTA Chennai, ready to take on her duties. There were 24 other female candidates that were selected. Little did they know what to expect and how the training was to happen because it was their first time.

Priya was trained with other female cadets, and they were not discriminated against by their male counterparts. They had to undergo rigorous training, and there was no leniency towards them.

Priya had stood out in a society where females are considered soft and inferior to men. She proved and paved the way for all those potential female candidates who want to serve in the defense services. She herself didn't know that the letter that she wrote would create such a big impact so big. It was her dream that she turned into reality. She is an inspiration to all those women who are still living their lives under the weight of the prejudice of society. She has proved that women are on par with men in every domain, and physical strength is no exception.

## Aruna Asraf Ali

Aruna Asraf Ali was born on July 16, 1909, in Kalka, Punjab. Her parents, Upendranath Ganguly and Ambaliks Devi, were followers of Brahmo Samaj. Her father was a restaurant owner, and they migrated from Barisal to the United Provinces of that time.

Aruna's parents were fairly liberal, and she had the opportunity to go to school. She did her schooling at Lahore's Sacred Heart Convent and completed her college education at All Saints' College in Nainital. She was one of the few women who used to complete their graduation. After her graduation, she worked as a teacher at Calcutta's Gokhale Memorial School. This was the time when she met her future husband, Asraf Ali.

The time when they got married, her father had passed away, and her uncle, who recognized himself as his guardian, was against the idea of 19-year-old Aruna marrying a man from another religion. Not just that Asraf Ali was 23 years older than her. In her biography, She has written how her uncle told her other family members that she was dead to him the moment she got married and how her uncle, Nagendranath Gangualy, performed her shraddh when she was alive.

Image- Aruna Asraf Ali
Image Source- The print

Despite her family being critical of her marriage, she stood by her decision to marry Asraf Ali.

Asraf Ali was a prominent lawyer and freedom fighter. He was closely associated with the Indian National Congress as well. Aruna Asraf Ali, because of her husband, got interested in politics. She became a prominent figure and took part in many national moments. After two years of her marriage, when she was 21, she was sent behind the bars for her involvement in the Salt Satyagraha. The charges against her were serious, and as a result, she wasn't released even after the Gandhi-Irwin pact of 1931, when all other prisoners were released.

The decision of the British government to keep Aruna in jail was because of her increasing image. But this decision backfired on the British government. Following the cancellation of Aruna's release, all other women inmates refused to get released in order to support Aruna. The public came in support of her, and it was after the personal intervention of Gandhi that she was released.

The next year, Aruna was again put in jail by the authorities, but they couldn't cage her ambitions. She started a hunger strike inside the jail, which was joined by other inmates as well. The strike was against the indifferent treatment that was being carried out. Britishers were fed up with her and moved her to the Ambala jail. But her strike was already a success when she noticed that the conditions had improved in the Ambala jail. She was released soon after.

She kept playing an active role in every possible way. A decade later, in 1942, she took a move that etched her name in Indian history. She was 33 years old when, in 1942, a full-fledged 'Quit India Movement' was initiated. The news made the British government furious, and they came down heavily on the leaders. As a consequence, all the major leaders, including Jawaharlal Nehru and Mahatma Gandhi, were arrested. This left the moment leaderless. 33-year-old Aruna here took the lead. She presided over the remaining sessions and even hoisted the Tricolor at the Gowalia Tank Maidan in Bombay. This was followed by massive protests and hartals in the city. The moment was alive even before any direct leadership because of her. She went underground after this move.

Even when she was underground, she was using radio, magazines, and newspapers like Inqualab to carry forward the moment. The British government was so frustrated because of her that they put a cash prize for whoever will tell about her. She met the socialist leaders like Jayaprakash Narayan, Ram Manohar Lohia, and Edatata Narayanan when she was hiding.

All the prisoners were later released, and Aruna was still underground. Her health was deteriorating, and Gandhi wrote her a handwritten letter that said, "I have been filled with admiration for your courage and heroism. You are reduced to a skeleton. Do come out and surrender yourself and win the prize offered for your arrest. Reserve the prize money for the Harijan [untouchables] cause.". This letter is framed and is present in her living room.

Soon after, she returned to political life at the behest of Mahatma Gandhi. Later, she even left the Congress Socialist Party to join the Communist Party of India (CPI).

In 1947, when India got independence, she began working on other issues that were persistent at that time, like women's empowerment and labor issues. In 1953, she faced a personal loss when Asaf Ali passed away. In 1958, she became the first elected mayor of Delhi, and she focused on bringing in major civil reforms. The political scenario was becoming petty, and she soon left the post and began to work on more newspaper-oriented reforms. In 1964, she was awarded the International Lenin Peace Prize, Padma Vibhushan in 1992, and the Bharat Ratna in 1997, a year after her death on July 29, 1996, at the age of 87.

## Savitribai Phule

Savitribai Phule was the woman who fought and played a pivotal role in the education of women. She was married at the age of 9, when she didn't know how to read and write. She was very attached to a book that she got from a Christian missionary. Her husband, Jyotiba Phule, who was himself 13 at the time, taught her how to read and write. This was when women had no position or say in society and when thought of being educated was only a dream for them.

It was at this time that Savitribai Phule undertook training at Ahmednagar and a school in Pune and became the first Indian woman teacher.

In 1848, both Jyotiba and his wife Savitribai Phule opened a school in Pune, Maharashtra. The school was open for girls belonging to all castes. She had already made a distinction by being an educated woman, and the idea of her going to the school to teach was not liked by the patriarchal society of the time. On her way to the school, she used to carry an extra pair of sarees, as the males of the society used to throw stones, mud, and even dung on her. But she was determined, and in 1851, after defying all the odds, she opened three schools. She even gave a stipend to the girls in order to prevent them from dropping out of school.

Image- Savitribai Phule
Source- Jagaran Josh

She worked against another evil that was prevalent in society against young widows, where they were harassed by their relatives and, on being pregnant, were left alone. Sabvitribai Phule, along with her husband, started a widow shelter. The widows were taken care of, and their babies were raised there. The couple adopted a child from that shelter as well.

Jyotibai Phule broke another societal taboo when she led the funeral procession of her husband. The rites, which even in today's world are considered sacred and are performed only by the males, were challenged by the fierce Jyotibai at that time.

She didn't care about her life and always did what she found was right. The strong woman never bowed down against the patriarchal society norms. She stood up for herself and worked for the depressed and harassed section of society.

## M. Fatima Beevi

M. Fatima Beevi, the woman who etched her name in Indian history, was born on 30 April 1927 in present-day Kerala. Born to Annaveetil Meera Sahib and Khadeeja Beevi, she was their eldest daughter. Fatima was a great learner and her father always supported all his kids to learn and study. She did her schooling from Catholicate High School in Pathanamthitta, Kerala. Her father was her source of motivation all the time. He supported her studies and as a result she completed her graduation in chemistry from University College, Trivandrum. She wanted to continue with her Masters in the same field but it was only because of her father that she went into Law college. Her father, who was a government servant, was inspired by Anna Cabdy who was the first female judicial officer working near Travancore, and wanted Fatima to do something big too. He knew that a masters degree would land her as a professor or teacher in Trivandrum only. He was ambitious and wanted Fatima to pursue law. She agreed with her father and joined Government Law College in Trivandrum.

She was one of the five women in her class, where the number was reduced to three the next year. This was the condition

Image- Justice M. Fatima Beevi

of the field when Fatima Beevi emerged as a role model for many. In a field that was dominated by men, she was the only woman there, and above all, she broke the barrier by getting a gold medal. It was her way of telling the world that women are no less than men. 1949-50. 14 November 1950, when she was enrolled as an advocate in the lower judiciary in Kollam, Kerala.

She was an outlier in the courts of the time. She was a woman lawyer who wore a headscarf in the courtroom. She obviously faced a lot of side eyes and comments, but she knew that she was doing it for her father, and she was strong enough to overcome all the obstacles that she faced in that field.

She was appointed as Munsiff in Kerala Subordinate Judicial Services in 1958 and was promoted as subordinate judge in 1968. She became Chief Judicial Magistrate in 1972 and then became the District and Sessions Judge in 1974. She was later appointed as the Judicial Member of the Income Tax Appellate Tribunal in 1980.

On May 14, 1984, she became a permanent judge of the High Court. It was on October 6, 1989, that she finally became the judge of the Supreme Court. She was the first women judge of the Supreme Court in India and the first women Muslim judge of Apex Court in Asia. In an interview with Scroll.in, she would say of this historic moment, 'I opened a closed door.

She retired from the apex court in 1992, after which she became the first woman member of the NHRC. She was then appointed as the Governor of Tamil Nadu from January 1997 to July 2001.

## Falguni Nayar

In the era where glass ceilings are prominent and women are still struggling to prove themselves capable of doing business and handling things well, Falguni Nayar, the CEO and founder of Nykaa, is an inspiration to many.

A bold and fierce woman who proved that age is not a barrier and had the courage to leave her well-established career to start something of her own.

Image- Falguni NayarImage
Source- The better india

Falguni Nyar was born in Mumbai on February 19, 1963, in a Gujarati family. As she grew up, she was inspired by her father's baking company. She found the business setups very lucrative and was inspired by the world of markets. As she grew up and completed her schooling, she decided to pursue her bachelor's in commerce. She took admission in Sydenham College of Commerce and Economics, and later she even completed her Master's from the Indian Institute of Management, Ahmadabad. This was where she met Sanjay Nayar. They both felt a connection and got married in 1987. They later had two kids, named Adwaita and Anchit Nayar. Life was going well, and she had a job in her. She was the managing director of the Kotak Mahindra Group in 2012.

She turned 50 at the time, and she was a little shy about her age, but her dream of becoming an entrepreneur was alive. She aspired to start a company, and in 2012, as a result, she resigned as Managing Director. She was scared, but she was determined. After gathering courage and reminding herself that age is nothing but a number, she started her own store and named it Nykaa.

The journey that Falguni was on had no petals on the way. In the first year of the establishment of Nykaa, it wasn't very lucrative or popular. She didn't have any people of her own and hired three people from her father's office. Later, her daughter joined the venture, and Falguni managed to get a small office, which was offered by her father. She, along with her daughter and three people on board, were taking care of everything. The brand saw a little growth in the first year. Nykaa was not performing exceptionally, but Mrs. Nayar didn't give up. In 2015, Nyka brought its line of cosmetic and beauty products into the market and became an instant hit! In the next four years, Nykaa saw immense growth and became the mightiest platforms in India. The dream of Falguni Naayar finally was becoming a reality. All her hard work paid off, and in 2020 Nykaa became the first women-led unicorn of India.

Even after more than seven decades of India's independence, women are subjected to discrimination on the basis of gender. They are subjected to social stigmas and are considered weak. The working women witness problems such as glass- ceilings even now, and they are considered a better fit for household chores and raising kids. Our government has to work and roll out schemes for the empowerment of women, but even after all the efforts, even though improvement has been seen, they are still falling behind when compared to other developing countries.

Falguni Nayar has set an example for all these women who themselves consider that after having children, their sole duty is to raise them. She became an inspiration to many and proved that women can be at par with men in every domain. She became an inspiration to many women in the contemporary world.

## Sara Thakral

India, which today has the highest percentage of women pilots in the world, once was not ready to accept women in the aviation sector. It was the time when women were thought to belong to the household chores only when a lady with the dream to touch the sky made history by becoming the first Indian woman to fly an aircraft—Sarla Thakral.

Sarla Thakral was born in 1914 in Delhi, the era of male-dominated society where female reformists were still soaring and women were trying to emerge as leaders with some successful examples. Sarla had an inclination towards the aviation industry since the beginning.

Image- Sara Thakral
Image Source- feminisminindia.com

The society was not liberal and Sarla was married to P.D. Thakral at a very tender age of 16. P.D. Thakara was himself a pilot and had 8 other pilots in the family, including his father. Sarla's dream saw a new push when she was encouraged by her father-in-law and husband to become a pilot. She was admitted to Lahore Flying Club at the age of 21, when she had a four-year-old daughter with her. This was a bold move that brought Sarla under the eye of society, which couldn't see a woman in a sector that was dominated by and thought to be belonging to the males only. Her training began, and after eight hours and ten minutes, her trainer asked her, "Are you ready to fly solo?". Sarla Thakral, wearing a saree, agreed. She demonstrated her skills and became an icon in 1936. She continued and moved forward in her journey with the wings, which were aired by the confidence and support of her husband. Between all the taunts and questions of the patriarchal world she was in, Sarla successfully completed 1000 hours of flight and finally bagged her 'A' licence. This was an accomplishment and fueled her zeal to get her 'B' license, which would allow her to fly a commercial plane.

Amid her journey and goal, she faced an unexpected setback: P.D. Thakral lost his life in an airplane crash in 1939. Sarla saw the world falling apart. It was a heavy loss for her, but she knew she couldn't give up. She recalled herself and left for Jodhpur for their training to become a commercial pilot license. Sarla was trying to absorb reality and was already on her way to achieve her goal when World War II broke out. The war made her career in aviation come to a halt. Sarla couldn't believe what was happening; she lost her husband, and then the war brought her dream to almost an end. But Sarla was not someone who would bow down in front of adversities. She decided to upskill herself and returned to Lahore. She received a diploma in fine arts from Mayo School of Art, and finally, when the partition happened, she came back to her hometown and her two daughters. She met with R.P. Thakral in Delhi and got married to him in 1948.

Sarla Thakral, who is known for becoming the first woman to fly a plane in India, is also a woman who had many other talents. She was a successful designer and a skilled painter too. All those women who are in the aviation sector, living their dream as a pilot, you owe her!

## Laxhmi Sehgal

Laxmi Sehgal, commonly referred to as Captain Laxhmi, was born on October 24, 1914, to a socially active family. Her father S. Swaminathan was a lawyer, and her mother

A.V. Ammukutty was a social activist. Both her parents were social workers, which is why Laxhmi had very liberal and progressive views. She used to question discriminatory practices from a very young age.

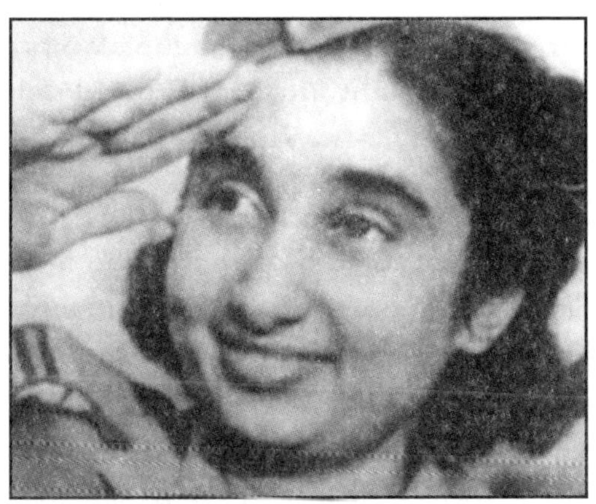

Image- Lakshmi Sehgal
Image Source- The better india

Her learned family provided her the opportunity to study, which was not available to most of the females at that time. Laxhmi did her schooling and joined Queen's Mary College in Madras in 1932, but she was married to P.K.B. Rao, a pilot at that time. The marriage was not successful, and Laxhmi moved back to her hometown. She clearly knew what he needed to do next. She decided to pursue MBBS in 1938 and got her diploma in gynecology and obstetrics in 1940. She later joined the Government Kasturba Gandhi Hospital, Madras.

But Laxhmi wanted to utilize her knowledge and experience to serve the people, and that is when she decided to move to Singapore, where she opened a clinic for migrant workers from India. That is when she even got associated with the Indian Independence League, which was led by Ras Behari Bose. Little did Laxhmi know that her decision to move to

Singapore would give her journey a new turn.

Singapore in 1942 witnessed Japanese occupation, and Laxhmi played her role as a doctor there. She served the prisoners of war and witnessed the effects of war very closely. Her association with the league also provided her with knowledge and insight into the situation of the world and India.

The next year, in 1943, Netaji Shubhash Bose visited Singapore and took the lead of the Indian Independence League from Ras Behari Bose. Laxhmi was impressed by Netaji's words and functioning and requested to join him, and she was allowed. She even became the only woman in Netaji's Council of Ministers in the provisional government of Azad Hind. In 1944, Laxhmi was appointed the commanding officer in the Rani Jhansi Regiment, an all-women regiment of the INA, which was moving from the Burma front. She was detained in Rangoon by the British because of her participation in INA, from where she was returned to India after a year.

On coming back, she started working to raise funds for the refugees on the INA. She even used to go and meet them in their camps, which were set in Madras. At this time she met Colonel Prem Kumar Sehgal, who was Captain in INA. They both decided to get married in 1946 and moved to Kanpur.

Even after her marriage, the urge to serve the country didn't leave Laxhmi. She served the people who were affected by the 1947 partition by setting up relief camps and medical aid, and even in the 1971 war. Sahgal joined the Communist Party of India (Marxist) and represented the party in the Rajya Sabha in the same year. She played an important role in restoring peace and harmony during the

1984 anti-Sikh riots. Apart from that, she set up a relief camp in Bhopal after the gas tragedy.

Dr. Laxhmi spent her whole life serving the country and its people. The hands that held bandages also held grenades at some time. She was always on the go when it came to community service. Sahgal was awarded the Padma Vibhushan in 1998 and bestowed with an honorary doctorate by the University of Calicut in 2010. A woman is not limited to the four walls; she can use weapons when needed and can serve the needy too.

## Sucheta Kriplani

In 1908, India was witnessing an increasing feeling of partition and riots and was grappling with the partition of Bengal. In Ambala, on June 25, Sucheta Kriplani was born. She grew up in an India that was not stable, and the idea of swaraj was getting firm. This environment had an impact on Sucheta and her sister Sulekha, and they both wanted to join India's independence movement.

Image- Sucheta Kriplani
Image Source- The better india

Sucheta completed her schooling, and her desire to serve the movement grew stronger. There is an incident which she has shared in the autobiography where she tells how she, along with her sister, was forced to stand near the Kudsia Garden to honor the Prince of Wales. Despite wanting to refuse, because of the Jallianwala Bagh massacre, they were forced to follow the instructions. This made her more furious, and she was filled with aggression against British Rule.

She later completed her education from Delhi's Indraprastha College. She was just 21 when she passed out, and she was ready to join the struggle. It was also the university where Sucheta met her future husband, Jivatram Bhagwandas Kripalani, who was another leader of the freedom movement. While Syucheta was looking for an opportunity to enter into the movement, she lost her sister and father in 1929. This came as a big blow to Sucheta's life. She was burdened with family responsibilities.

In 1938, Sucheta and Acharaya Kripalani decided to tie the knot. Their decision was opposed by both the families and even Mahatma Gandhi. But regardless of all the odds, they both were determined to marry each other. Acharaya Ji was 20 years older than Sucheta, which was a big reason for her family's denial of her marriage. She even started her professional career in 1939 as a teacher at Banaras Hindu University.

With Acharaya Kriplani by her side, Sucheta stepped into the political arena. She progressed her career and, in 1940, founded the Indian National Congress Women's Wing along with the All India Mahila Congress. She had a deep respect and regard for Mahatma Gandhi and was a strong follower of Gnadhian principles. She was also an active participant in the Quit India Movement of 1942, for which she was imprisoned for a year. Her dedication and activeness in national politics and movements opened different gates for her. One such being the Constituent Assembly. She was elected to the Assembly from the United Povience and was a member of the Flag Presentation Committee.

In 1947, when India got its hard-earned independence, both Sucheta and Archaraya were involved in a relief camp in Noakhali, which was the worst affected region because of the partition.

Sucheta was one of the first few women who were parliamentarians in Independent India and was even the part of several delegations to foreign countries and organizations like the Parliamentary Delegation to Turkey, 1954; the United Nations General Assembly, 1949, etc. She also acted as the Chief Minister of Uttar Pradesh from 1963 to 1967, where she dealt with the economic downfall of the state. She was a Lok Sabha from Gonda in Uttar Pradesh and finally retired from politics in 1971.

## Myths And Facts

While growing up in an Indian society, I heard of many restrictions and rules that a woman undergoing her menstrual cycle should follow Not only that, I even saw females being restricted to join the cremation ground and the last rites. There are different myths and taboos surrounding the life of women. They have been followed for centuries. But do you know the reason why these myths originated? Ever thought, do they make any sense in contemporary society?

Let us discuss some of them here

## Can Touching Food Or Pickles During Periods Spoil It?

"Don't touch the food! You will spoil it." You must have heard this as a woman. Even if you are a male, you would have heard such lines once every month. When a woman gets menstruation, it is a common belief that whatever food she touches, especially pickles, gets spoiled. But is this true? Well, not really.

Let's first understand what causes food spoilage. Spoilage of food happens because of the microorganisms that degrade it. They can be bacteria, fungi, or anything. While food can also spoil because of weather factors, here we will focus on the microbes. These members of the microbiota are attracted by the unhygienic conditions. In ancient times, women used to use cloth to manage hygiene. It was definitely not a really good absorber and thereby caused hygiene issues. Women in those days therefore abstained from touching any sort of food.

With the evolution of time, we have advanced in the domain of menstrual hygiene. We have seen the coming of menstrual pads, intimate hygiene washes, and hand washes in pictures. These products are made to prioritize hygiene. Therefore, in today's world, we have more products available and fewer chances of food spoilage.

But in certain rural and backward areas, we still find women using clothes. Partly because they are in the shackles of ancient practices and partly because of the economic factor.

So you see, food spoilage is not because of periods, per say. It is because of the hygiene factor, which has gained popularity and improved over the period of time. Therefore, a woman maintaining hygiene can simply touch the food, and yes, it won't spoil.

## Do Not Sweep After Sunset

There is another very common myth that is deeply rooted in India: women shouldn't sweep after sunset. Why? It is believed that Mata Laxmi, the goddess of wealth and prosperity, pays a visit in the evening. Women sweeping the house after sunset upsets her. This leads to a degrading wealth condition for the family.

So is this true? Absolutely not. Then where did this myth come from? This is because of the absence of technological advancement in ancient India.

The LEDs and tubelights that are readily available to our generation were absent in ancient India. As a result, people relied upon kerosene lamps or candles. Women adorned with gold jewelry faced the risk of accidentally discarding delicate pieces like nose pins while sweeping. The lack of proper lighting made such mishaps very common.

But now, we live in a modern world with all the facilities. We don't carry any risks for such mishaps. Therefore, we shouldn't worry about Mata Laxmi being upset.

**THE END**

THE END

Dear readers,

As a kid, I saw a world where women were considered inferior to men in different aspects of life. But as I grew up, I often found myself grappling with questions like, "Was it really like this? Were women truly the feeble beings they're often portrayed as today?" In my own life, I've seen women manage households, nurture families, and juggle countless responsibilities. This realization made me curious to delve deeper into the true histories of women. And now, as I conclude this journey, I want to reflect on the profound experiences that have shaped this book. Initially, it was just an idea swirling in my mind, and now, holding this completed work fills me with fulfillment.

Throughout this process, I aimed to highlight remarkable women whose stories of struggle and bravery are often overlooked. While I couldn't include every name, I want to acknowledge a few inspiring figures: Tara Rani Srivastava, Rani Chennabhairadevi, Velu Nachiyar, Rani Avantibai of Ramgarh, Laal Ded, Jijabai, and Basanti Devi, among many others. Their contributions remind us that countless women have fought for recognition and deserve to be celebrated.

I had an idea with me and before diving into the writing, I gathered with my incredible team and my developmental editor, Raveena Paul, to brainstorm. At that stage, the concept was raw and needed direction. So to build a foundation, we had extensive discussions, sharing our scattered ideas. Out of all the discussion that we had, one key realization emerged: while many people are familiar with the negative aspects of feminism, the positive contributions are often overlooked. We felt it was essential to highlight the uplifting and empowering narratives that have faded over time.

Driven by this insight, I embarked on a deep research journey. I sifted through books, articles, and scholarly papers, determined to unveil stories that debunk the myths surrounding female identity. Initially skeptical, I often found references to women without celebrating their strength. My exploration took me back to the roots, diving into the Vedas, Upanishads, and other sacred texts. Though I'm not a Sanskrit scholar, the English translations offered new insights, revealing the sacred status of women and strengthening my resolve to share their stories.

This research journey was long and challenging—it took us ten months to explore the aspects of feminism. There were days of disheartenment when solid evidence felt elusive, and moments when I questioned the feasibility of this project. I remember days slipping away in the depths of research, with daily Google Meets and endless exchanges of ideas and queries. Each discussion brought us closer to clarity, transforming raw ideas into a structured narrative.

Yet, this journey was rewarding in its own right. We unearthed concepts that are crucial yet often overlooked, many of which resonate in today's world. One such idea, my personal favorite, is the spiritual equality of all beings, emphasizing that at the spiritual level, men and women are equal. Best part? It is written in the ancient texts themselves, the sacred source of our understanding.

As a researcher and as a human being, this experience has been enriching and deeply satisfying. I want to extend my heartfelt gratitude to you, dear readers, for your time, love, and support. It truly means the world to me. I hope this book brings you joy and insight, just as writing it has brought me.

Thank you.

# Citations


## CHAPTER - 1

*https://prabhupadabooks.com/sb/9/10/54* **-eka-patnivrata dharma**

*https://www.academia.edu/38133191/From_Nautch_Girl_to_Tawaif_converted_pdf* **-Twaiffs**

*https://news.nd.edu/news/woman-the-hunter-studies-aim-to-correct-history/#:~:text=The%20female%20body%20structure%20itself,their%20steps%2C%E2%80%9D%20Ocobock%20detailed.* **-women were never inferior to men**

## CHAPTER - 2

**- Stone age was a hard time, everybody needed to work because there were not enough hands to do the tasks**

*https://study.com/academy/lesson/roles-of-women-in-the-stone-age.html*

**- Equality is what differentiates us from our primate cousins. Humanity started with gender equality and its segregation was never natural**

*https://www.theguardian.com/science/2015/may/14/early-men-women-equal-scientists* **-Women hunted**

*https://www.nytimes.com/2023/08/01/science/anthropology-women-hunting.html* **-men and women hunted together**

*https://www.deccanherald.com/science/prehistoric-women-engaged-in-hunting-their-anatomy-suitable-for-it-us-researchers-2785420*

**-women physiology-advantage because of bigger pelvis and estrogen in the body.**

*https://news.nd.edu/news/woman-the-hunter-studies-aim-to-correct-history/#:~:text=The%20female%20body%20structure%20itself,their%20steps%2C%E2%80%9D%20Ocobock%20detailed.*

**-no difference in trauma patterns between males and females, because they were doing the same activities**

*https://www.eurekalert.org/news-releases/1005447#:~:text=%E2%80%9CWhen%20we%20take%20a%20deeper,people%20lived%20in%20small%20groups.*

**-Children were raised together and was a communal affair**

*https://www.euronews.com/culture/2023/11/15/study-reveals-stone-age-babies-belonging-to-tribes-may-have-received-better-parenting*

*https://psycnet.apa.org/fulltext/2024-21265-001.html*

**-Skin to skin contact -3/4 th fingerprints on the caves were of women signifying that they had a significant position in society.**

*https://www.nationalgeographic.com/adventure/article/131008-women-handprints-oldest-neolithic-cave-art*

*https://journals.plos.org/plosone/article?id=10.1371/journal.pone.0287101&trk=public_post_comment-text* **-Study by Dr. Wall-Scheffler**

*https://www.iflscience.com/women-may-be-better-hunters-than-men-latest-research-argues-71719* **-Research paper by Cara Ocobock for traumatic injuries**

*https://www.scientificamerican.com/article/the-theory-that-*

*men-evolved-to-hunt-and-women-evolved-to-gather-is-wrong1/* **-Study by Cara Ocobock and Sara Lacy for estrogen**

## Image sources

*https://www.nytimes.com/2023/08/01/science/anthropology-women-hunting.html* **-Excavations**

*https://www.nationalgeographic.com/adventure/article/131008-women-handprints-oldest-neolithic-cave-art* **-Hand prints**

*https://ms.fortresspress.com/downloads/0800697901Chapter1.pdf* **-IVC**

*https://sindhishaan.com/gallery/female_fig.html -Nursing infant*

*https://telibrary.com/wp-content/uploads/2022/08/IVC_religion_by_Naga_Ganesan_2007.pdf* **-Indus Narrative Tablet**

*https://www.speakingtree.in/blog/tiger-goddess-of-indus-valley* **-Tiger Godess**

*https://www.harappa.com/sites/default/files/pdf/Kenoyer1992_Ornament%20Styles%20of%20the%20Indus%20Valley%20Tradition%20Ev.pdf - Ornament styles*

## CHAPTER - 3

**Figurines-** *http://www.people.vcu.edu/~djbromle/artviewsnet/portrait04/jithin/indusvalley.htm*

## Gender and sex in Indus valley

*https://core.ac.uk/download/pdf/5105465.pdf*

*https://core.ac.uk/download/pdf/5105465.pdf*

*https://ncert.nic.in/textbook/pdf/kefa102.pdf* **-NCERT**

**further supporting the fact that both men and women wore ornaments during Harappan times.**

**Tiger goddess-** *https://www.mid-day.com/news/opinion/article/tigress-goddess-of-harappa-23216100#*

*https://telibrary.com/wp-content/uploads/2022/08/IVC_religion_by_Naga_Ganesan_2007.pdf*

## People of Indus valley

*http://iks.iitgn.ac.in/wp-content/uploads/2017/01/Peoples-and-Professions-in-Indus-Civilization-JM-Kenoyer.pdf*

*https://core.ac.uk/download/pdf/5105465.pdf#:~:text=adult%20women%2C%20but%20not%20men%2C%20are%20sometimes,of%20production%20and%20provide%20a%20different%20perception. - Women and wealth*

## Contemporary matrilineal societies-

*https://nesac.gov.in/assets/resources/2020/12/Interpretation-of-womens-Role_An-analysis-on-Khasi-tribe-of-Meghalaya.pdf* **-Khasi community**

*https://www.bbc.com/travel/article/20210328-why-some-indians-want-more-mens-rights* **-Ka khadduh**

*https://www.google.com/url?q=https://eastjaintiahills.gov.in/the-people/%23:~:text%3DJaintias%2520are%2520a%2520matrilineal%2520society,family%2520is%2520always%2520the%2520father.&sa=D&source=docs&ust=1730-124340284220&usg=AOvVaw36GuYHQRfQKI2jq6u5Tr0c* **-Jaintia community**

*https://www.arfjournals.com/image/catalog/Journals%20Papers/MII/2020/No.3-4/06.pdf* **-Minicoy matrilineal culture**

*https://www.blindian-project.com/post/kerala-matriarchy#:~:text=The%20Nayars%20/%20Nairs%20* **-Matrilineal community in south india.**

*https://sanipanhwar.com/uploads/books/2024-08-29_12-21-48_c25d5e87cf5299970e3ea7d62068607f.pdf* **-Presence of Citadel in Mohenjo-daro**

*https://www.britannica.com/topic/Indus-civilization* **-Great bath**

*https://theindosphere.com/history/sophistication-of-the-indus-valley/* **-Pashupati seal**

## Religious beliefs of people of IVC

*https://www.researchgate.net/publication/370954363_The_Supposed_Religious_Beliefs_of_the_Indus_Valley_Civilization_-_Revised_in_View_of_Recent_Research*

*https://www.researchgate.net/publication/384051488_Indus_Valley_Civilization_Reading*

*https://theindosphere.com/history/sophistication-of-the-indus-valley/*

*https://sanipanhwar.com/uploads/books/2024-08-29_12-21-48_c25d5e87cf5299970e3ea7d62068607f.pdf*

## Image sources

*http://www.rhinoresourcecenter.com/pdf_files/129/1290844154.pdf* **-Great bath**

*https://www.bibhudevmisra.com/2016/01/shiva-as-bada-dev-gond-symbolisms-on 23.html* **-Pashupati seal** *https://www.harappa.com/blog/unicorn-and-pipal-tree-seal* **-Pipal seal**

## CHAPTER - 4

*https://www.google.com/url?q=https://www.journalppw.com/index.php/jpsp/article/download/3256/2116/3712&sa=D&source=docs&ust=1730124700489130&usg=AOvVaw2VeeQ8wiAPdpF1N2D_U-Rw* **-Brihaddharam Purana**

**Women in Epics and Upanishads-** *http://oldsite.pup.ac.in/e-content/social_sciences/home_sc/MHomescience42.pdf*

**Women in Vedic age-** *https://archive.org/details/dli.ernet.506179- Book*

**Women in Sacred Laws-** *https://archive.org/details/dli.ernet.536771/page/n7/mode/2up- Book*

**Role and Position of Women : An Exploration Through Rig-Veda** *ijsrst.com/paper/6869.pdf*

**Indian feminism in vedic perspective-** *https://vedicheritage.gov.in/pdf/Indian_Feminism_in_Vedic_Perspective.pdf*

**Feminism in Vedic era-** *https://www.youtube.com/watch?v=e9FaC-kC-cA*

**Talk on Vedic feminism-** *https://www.vifindia.org/event/report/2021/january/27/talk-on-vedic-feminism*

**Gandharva marriage-** *https://www.weddingwire.in/wedding-tips/gandharva-marriage--c2845*

**Myth of Sati-** *https://www.academia.edu/45549368/Vedas_Not_for_Sati*

*https://vedicvishal.wordpress.com/2021/04/09/myth-of-sati/*

**Saptapadi-** *https://www.thetamarindtree.in/blog/saptapadi-*

*saat-phere/*

*https://www.astroyogi.com/wedding/saptapadi*

*https://hindupriestketuljoshi.co.uk/saptpadi-and-seven-vows-of-hindu-wedding/#:~:text=%E2%80%9COm%20esha%20ekapadi%20bhava%20iti,your%20basic%20needs%20are%20fulfilled.*

*https://papers.ssrn.com/sol3/papers.cfm?abstract_id=3512976*

*Abortions and contraceptives- https://enrouteindianhistory.com/abortions-contraceptives-and-womens-health-in-ancient-india/*

## Image sources

*https://www.journalppw.com/index.php/jpsp/article/download/3256/2116/3712* **-Women in vedas**

*https://www.britannica.com/topic/Ardhanarishvara* **- Ardhanareshwar**

## CHAPTER -5

**More on women in ancient India and during Mauryans-** *https://enrouteindianhistory.com/?s=women*

*https://www.academia.edu/39787204/Upanishads_the_Source_of_Indian_Spiritual_Manifestations* **-Upanishads as ultimate source**

## CHAPTER 6

**Ganga-** *https://archive.org/details/the-palace-of-illusions-com-v4-0/page/n161/mode/2up?view=theater*

**Draupadi-** *https://draupadiparashakti.com/draupadi-story/*

## Satyavati

*https://www.dnaindia.com/lifestyle/column-satyavati-the-feminist-who-stood-up-to-patriarchy-2475404* **-Referred article**

*https://www.scribd.com/document/510247164/The-Fisher-Queen-s-Dynasty-by-Kavita-Kane-1* **-Referred Book for knowing the early life of Satyavati.**

*https://archive.org/details/panditaramabaist00dyer_0/page/n19/mode/2up?view=theater* **-A deeper understanding of her early life.**

## CHAPTER - 7

**Samana Festival-** *https://ijsrst.com/paper/6869.pdf*

*https://www.scribd.com/document/437360353/Prostitution-during-mauryan-empire-A-focus-on-Kautilya-s-views#:~:text=3.-,Prostitutes%20were%20supervised%20by%20officials%2C%20paid%20different%20salaries%20based%20on,tax%20revenue%20for%20the%20state.* **-Ganikas**

*https://www.google.com/url?q=https://enrouteindianhistory.com/women-in-the-mauryan-empire/&sa=D&source=docs&ust=1730125401874899&usg=AOvVaw1crYcT1Xqp1xuD3tFgRq5O* **-Prostitution in Mauryan empire**

*https://archive.org/details/in.gov.ignca.46370/page/n103/mode/2up?view=theater* **-Women in the Mauryan period**

**Gandharva vivah-** *https://www.weddingwire.in/wedding-tips/gandharva-marriage--c2845*

*https://www.hindustantimes.com/books/back-to-the-future-marriage-and-live-in-relationships-in-ancient-india-101712156618314.html https://www.wisdomlib.org/hinduism/essay/kamashastra-discourse-life-in-ancient-india/d/doc1239441.html#:~:text=In%20order%20of%20importance%2C%20the,the%20result%20of%20previous%20love.* **-kamasutra in favour of gandharva vivah**

*https://en.wikisource.org/wiki/Arthashastra/Book_III*

*https://www.wisdomlib.org/hinduism/essay/kamashastra-discourse-life-in-ancient-india/d/doc1239442.html* **-Kamasutra on widow remmariage**

*https://www.cambridge.org/core/journals/journal-of-law-and-religion/article/abs/property-rights-of-hindu-women-a-feminist-review-of-succession-laws-of-ancient-medieval-and-modern-india/A054D9949BF2EF6DC892C227B23A4476* **-Stridhan first mentioned in Manusmriti**

## CHAPTER - 8

*https://archive.org/details/in.gov.ignca.46370/page/n103/mode/2up?view=theater- Book*

**Nur jahan-** *https://digitalcommons.georgiasouthern.edu/cgi/viewcontent.cgi?article=1023&context=aujh*

*https://www.britannica.com/biography/Nur-Jahan*

**Begum Samru-** *https://storytrails.in/history/begum-samru-the-story-of-indias-only-christian-queen/*

*https://www.google.com/url?q=https://storytrails.in/history/begum-samru-the-story-of-indias-only-christian-queen/&sa=D&source=docs&ust=1730125749795753&usg=AOvVaw06675Y_fRlMiFLWkTnwhaA*

**Gulbadan Begum-** *https://www.atlasobscura.com/articles/mughal-princess-gulbadan-begum-author*

*https://www.google.com/url?q=https://www.ijnrd.org/papers/IJNRD2204124.sg=AOvVaw2nUgAFFh1o_4QQiZXbPlMD - Mecca*

**Rani Durgavati-** *https://indianculture.gov.in/stories/rani-durgavati*

**Naiki Devi-** *https://thebetterindia.com/143628/naiki-devi-chalukya-queen-gujarat-goa-defeat-muhammad-ghori/ https://www.opindia.com/2022/03/rani-naiki-devi-a-brave-queen-of-chalukyas-who-defeated-muhammad-ghori/#google_vignette*

**Rani Durgavati-** *https://indianculture.gov.in/stories/rani-durgavati*

*https://www.google.com/url?q=https://pib.gov.in/PressReleseDetailm.*

*source=docs&ust=1730125899309294&usg=AOvVaw3Gd_OanOpUDJdsDpSeeJDJ* **-postal stamp**

*https://commons.wikimedia.org/wiki/File:Delivery_of_ICGS_Rani_Durgavati.jpg* **-ICGS Rani Durgavati**

## Image sources

*https://digitalcommons.georgiasouthern.edu/cgi/viewcontent.cgi?article=1023&context=aujh* **-Nur Jahan**

*http://www.punjabjalandhar.info/2009/04/nurmahal-sarai-western-lahori-gate.html* **-Inscriptions**

*https://en.wikipedia.org/wiki/Zeb-un-Nissa#/media/File:A_Bejeweled_Maiden_with_a_Parakeet.jpg - Zeb-un-Nissa*

*https://en.wikipedia.org/wiki/Mirabai#/media/File:Kangra_painting_of_Mirabai,_the_female_Bhakti_saint.jpg* **-Mirabai**

*https://en.wikipedia.org/wiki/Kittur_Chennamma#/media/File:Kittur_Chenamma.jpg* **-Rani Channaman**

## CHAPTER - 9

**Women in Harem-** *https://scroll.in/article/1036525/domesticity-and-power-in-the-early-mughal-world-ruby-lal-challenges-the-fantasies-about-the-harem#:~:text=While%20the%20haram%20may%20have,Permanent%20Black%20and%20Ashoka%20University.*

*https://www.google.com/url?q=https://archive.org/details/in.gov.ignca.46370/page/n103/mode/2up?view%3Dtheater&sa=D&source=docs&ust=1730126029801242&usg=AOvVaw0tjuggBsk-ZvdH5volWS8m* **-book**

*https://www.hansshodhsudha.com/volume2-issue4/Manuscript%209.pdf* **-Chingizi Timurid culture**

*https://cognizancejournal.com/vol4issue3/V4I313.pdf* **-Euchus and financial resources**

*https://feminisminindia.com/2017/03/17/razia-sultan-essay/* **-Raziya Sultan**

**Makhfi-**

*https://ijrcs.org/wp-content/uploads/IJRCS201912010.pdf*

*https://archive.org/details/in.gov.ignca.46370/page/n103/mode/2up?view=theater*

**Angiya Kurti-** *https://feminisminindia.com/2018/10/19/zaib-un-nissa-princess/*

*https://feminisminindia.com/2018/10/19/zaib-un-nissa-princess/*

**Bhakti Movement-** *https://www.mainstreamweekly.net/article8630.html*

## Chapter 10- Women of south india

*https://feminisminindia.com/2019/11/08/rudrama-devi-queen-kings-image/* **-Rudrama devi**

*https://www.google.com/url?q=https://www.jetir.org/papers/JETIR2010014.*

*116069&usg=AOvVaw27WqG6QCmwUM2NRMBNVBjH* **-Chalukyas of Kalyan**

**Rani Chnnamma-** *https://ijcrt.org/papers/IJCRT1135018.pdf https://pib.gov.in/newsite/printrelease.aspx?relid=148944*

## CHAPTER - 11

**Associations in modern India-** *https://scholarcommons.scu.edu/cgi/viewcontent.cgi?article=1030&context=gender* **-All Indian women's conference**

*https://scholarcommons.scu.edu/cgi/viewcontent.cgi?article=1030&context=gender*

*https://scholarcommons.scu.edu/cgi/viewcontent.cgi?article=1030&context=gender* **-women's India association**

*https://epgp.inflibnet.ac.in/epgpdata/uploads/epgp_content/women_studies/gender_studies/03._women_and_history/17._history_of_womens_organisations_in_india/et/7886_et_et_17.pdf* **-National council of women in india**

**Literary sources**

*https://scholarworks.gsu.edu/cgi/viewcontent.cgi?article=1058&context=history_theses* **-Stri Dharma**

*https://highcourtchd.gov.in/hclscc/subpages/pdf_files/5.pdf* **-Sharda act**

*https://indiankanoon.org/doc/80896406/* **-Deshmukh bill**

*https://www.allsubjectjournal.com/assets/archives/2022/vol9issue11/9-9-54-466.pdf* **-Arya Mahila**

*https://ijcrt.org/papers/IJCRT2211027.pdf* *- Ghara Jeuti*

## Tribal women-

*https://www.researchgate.net/publication/327009025_Rani_Gaidinliu_The_Iconic_Woman_of_Northeast_India* **- Rani Gaidinliu**

*https://cmsadmin.amritmahotsav.nic.in/unsung-heroes-detail.htm?56*

*https://pibindia.wordpress.com/2015/09/30/rani-gaidinliu-daughter-of-the-hills/*

*https://magazines.odisha.gov.in/orissareview/2015/August/engpdf/august%20or%202015.pdf* **-Bângarâ Devi**

*https://magazines.odisha.gov.in/orissareview/April2006/engpdf/freedom_struggle_%20and%20rama%20devi_.pdf* **-Rama devi**

*https://amritmahotsav.nic.in/unsung-heroes-detail.htm?297* **-Malati Chaudhury**

*https://cmsadmin.amritmahotsav.nic.in/unsung-heroes-detail.htm?4552* **-Kuntal Kumari Sabat**

*https://amritmahotsav.nic.in/district-reopsitory-detail.htm?3056* **-Sarala devi**

*https://amritmahotsav.nic.in/unsung-heroes-detail.htm?4511* **-Jambubati Pattnaik**

## Women framing the constitution

**Ammu Swaminathan-** *https://cdgi.edu.in/pdf/Women_who_contributed_to_Indian_Constitution.pdf*

*https://www.google.com/url?q=https://feminisminindia.com/2018/09/04/ammu-swaminathan-freedom-fighter/&sa=D&source=docs&ust=1730126784191846&usg=AOvVaw3dfFQOgQBo7iDqqelK97gA*

*https://feminisminindia.com/2018/09/04/ammu-swaminathan-freedom-fighter/*

*Dakshayani Velayudhan - https://cdgi.edu.in/pdf/Women_who_contributed_to_Indian_Constitution.pdf*

*Begum Aizaz Rasul - https://cdgi.edu.in/pdf/Women_who_contributed_to_Indian_Constitution.pdf*

*https://newindiasamachar.pib.gov.in/WriteReadData/story/2021/Nov/S202111162877.pdf* **-15 women in constitution making**

## CHAPTER - 12

**Dr. Rakhmabai-** *https://feminisminindia.com/2017/08/22/rukhmabai-essay/-*

*https://www.google.com/url?q=https://indianliberals.in/gj/content/rukhmabai-an-unrelenting-force-against-patriarchal-norms/&sa=D&source=docs&ust=1730126941601359&usg=AOvVaw0txwTGIHsxM4oKP1kuQt5U*

*https://www.tandfonline.com/doi/full/10.1080/24730580.2021.1962083* **-2000 rupees for settlement**

*https://thebetterindia.com/65696/india-first-practising-lady-doctor-rukhmabai/#google_vignette*

*https://scroll.in/article/1063583/the-child-bride-who-challenged-patriarchy-and-became-one-of-indias-pioneering-women-doctors*

**Tarabai Shinde-** *https://thebetterindia.com/135270/me-too-19th-century-feminist-tarabai-shinde/*

*https://www.impriindia.com/insights/tarabai-shinde-women-empowerment/*

*https://sansad.in/getFile/loksabhaquestions/annex/8/AU1039.pdf?source=pqals* **-MP and Rajasthan**

*https://pib.gov.in/PressReleasePage.aspx?PRID=1806605#:~:text=As%20per%20the%20latest%205,sex%20ratio%20urban%20at%20985.* **-women, half of the population**

*https://pib.gov.in/PressReleaseIframePage.aspx?PRID=1944287 - NEP*

**Pandita Ramabai-** *https://www.google.com/url?q=https://indianliberals.in/gj/content/pandita-ramabai-a-trailblazing-feminist/&sa=D&source=docs&ust=1730127136118977&usg=AOvVaw0yRX5DmGEaer5TEqLnc8Jk*

*https://archive.org/details/panditaramabaist00dyer_0/page/n47/mode/2up* **-book**

**Priya Jhingham-** *https://thebetterindia.com/117015/first-woman-indian-army-priya-jhingan/*

*https://www.bharat-rakshak.com/army/personnel/women/always-001/#:~:text=When%20the%20full%2Dpage%20advertisement,Academy%20(OTA)%20in%20Chennai.*

*https://www.shethepeople.tv/interviews/first-woman-cadet-indian-army-major-priya-jhingan-interview-2400592* **-they were not discriminated**

*https://www.google.com/url?q=https://www.majorpriyajhingan.com/about-major-priya.n%2520Army&sa=D&source=docs&ust=1730127197114765&usg=AOvVaw3NJ_28lL8akNQc9DDJ4skW*

**Aruna Asraf Ali-** *https://theprint.in/theprint-profile/aruna-asaf-ali-a-fiercely-independent-freedom-fighter-who-defied-*

*mahatma-gandhi/90230/*

*https://theprint.in/theprint-profile/aruna-asaf-ali-a-fiercely-independent-freedom-fighter-who-defied-mahatma-gandhi/90230/* **-Shraddh**

**Savtribai Phule-** *https://www.google.com/url?q=https://historified.in/2024/05/10/savitribai-phule-introduction-to-feminism-women-education-and-reformations/&sa=D&source=docs&ust=1730127318105497&usg=AOvVaw1ICGlK41Bjnzd oQNKRoD_h*

*https://historified.in/2024/05/10/savitribai-phule-introduction-to-feminism-women-education-and-reformations/* **-she carried an extra saree**

*https://www.jagranjosh.com/general-knowledge/savitribai-phule-biography-husband-children-work-for-girls-education-schools-awards-death-1641193310-1*

*https://www.jagranjosh.com/general-knowledge/savitribai-phule-biography-husband-children-work-for-girls-education-schools-awards-death-1641193310-1*

**M Fatima Beevi-** *https://theprint.in/pageturner/excerpt/i-opened-a-closed-door-fathima-beevi-indias-1st-woman-judge-in-sc-who-remains-an-enigma/862301/*

*https://www.barandbench.com/columns/women-in-indian-judiciary-remembering-justice-m-fathima-beevi-part-i* **-gold medal**

*https://economictimes.indiatimes.com/news/india/justice-fathima-beevi-small-town-girl-who-breached-glass-ceiling-to-become-first-woman-sc-judge/articleshow/105450302.cms?from=mdr*

*https://www.padmaawards.gov.in/Document/pdf/CitationsForTickets/2024/20246.pdf*

**Falguni Nayar-** *https://www.google.com/url?q=https://thebetterindia.com/265560/nykaa-ipo-falguni-nayar-unicorn-billionaire-woman-entrepreneur-india/%23google_e&sa=D&source=docs&ust=1730127470265995&usg=AOvVaw2UAaTfqifDS1dVmAqqmlm-*

*https://www.cheggindia.com/earn-online/nykaa-founder-success-story/*

*https://www.ceotodaymagazine.com/2024/09/falguni-nayar-the-inspirational-success-story-of-nykaas-founder/*

**Sara Thakral-** *https://feminisminindia.com/2019/09/23/sarla-thakral-indias-first-woman-fly-aircraft/*

*https://www.aviationfile.com/sarla-thakral-the-first-indian-woman-to-fly-an-aircraft/#:~:text=In%20a%20time%20when%20the,others%20to%20follow%20her%20trail.* **-Lahore flying club**

*https://thebetterindia.com/18871/11-interesting-things-you-probably-didnt-know-about-indias-first-woman-pilot/#google_vignette - 1000 hours of flo=ight*

**Lakxmi Sehgal-** *https://thebetterindia.com/11547/doctor-freedom-fighter-activist-feminist-inspiring-woman-lakshmi-sehgal/#google_vignette*

*https://archives.ashoka.edu.in/paper_details/70#:~:text=Sahgal%20was%20one%20of%20the,gas%20tragedy%20in%20December%201984.*

**Sucheta Kriplani-** *https://archives.ashoka.edu.in/paper_details/70#:~:text=Sahgal%20was%20one%20of%20the,gas%20tragedy%20in%20December%201984.*

*https://cmsadmin.amritmahotsav.nic.in/district-reopsitory-detail.htm?32*

## Myths And Facts

*https://timesofindia.indiatimes.com/life-style/food-news/why-were-women-not-allowed-to-touch-pickles-during-periods/photostory/91814731.cms?picid=91882414 - spoilage of pickles*

*https://takeoffwithme.com/common-superstitions-in-india/* **-sweeping the floor after sunset**

## Image sources

*https://pibindia.wordpress.com/2015/09/30/rani-gaidinliu-daughter-of-the-hills/* **-Rani Gidinliu**

*https://magazines.odisha.gov.in/orissareview/April2006/engpdf/freedom_struggle_%20and%20rama%20devi_.pdf* **-Rama Devi**

*https://amritmahotsav.nic.in/unsung-heroes-detail.htm?297* **-Malati Choudhury**

*https://cmsadmin.amritmahotsav.nic.in/unsung-heroes-detail.htm?4552* **-Kuntala Kumari Sabat**

*https://amritmahotsav.nic.in/district-reopsitory-detail.htm?3056* **-Sarala devi**

*https://amritmahotsav.nic.in/unsung-heroes-detail.htm?4544* **-Jmabubati Pattnaik**

*https://cdgi.edu.in/pdf/Women_who_contributed_to_Indian_Constitution.pdf* **-Ammu Swaminathan**

*https://www.constitutionofindia.net/members/dakshayani-velayudhan/* **-Dakshayani Velayudhan**

*https://blog.ipleaders.in/a-woman-to-remember-begum-aizaz-rasul/* **-Begum Aizal Rasul**

*https://feminisminindia.com/2017/08/22/rukhmabai-essay/*

**-Dr. Rukhmabai**

*https://www.impriindia.com/insights/tarabai-shinde-women-empowerment/* **-Tarabai Shinde**

*https://indianliberals.in/gj/content/pandita-ramabai-a-trailblazing-feminist/* **-Pandita ramabai**

*https://www.majorpriyajhingan.com/about-major-priya.php#:~:text=Priya%20Jhingan%20was%20instrumental%20in,to%20join%20the%20Indian%20Army.* **-Priya jhingham**

*https://theprint.in/theprint-profile/aruna-asaf-ali-a-fiercely-independent-freedom-fighter-who-defied-mahatma-gandhi/90230/* **-The print**

*https://www.jagranjosh.com/general-knowledge/savitribai-phule-biography-husband-children-work-for-girls-education-schools-awards-death-1641193310-1* **-Savitribai Phule**

*https://thebetterindia.com/265560/nykaa-ipo-falguni-nayar-unicorn-billionaire-woman-entrepreneur-india/#google_vignette* **-Falguni Nayar**

*https://feminisminindia.com/2019/09/23/sarla-thakral-indias-first-woman-fly-aircraft/* **-Sara thakral**

*https://thebetterindia.com/11547/doctor-freedom-fighter-activist-feminist-inspiring-woman-lakshmi-sehgal/#google_vignette* **-Laxmi Sehgal**

*https://thebetterindia.com/198291/india-first-woman-cm-freedom-fighter-sucheta-kriplani/#google_vignette* **-Sucheta Kriplani**